GW00375295

Cambridge First Certificate in English 3

Official examination papers from University of Cambridge ESOL Examinations

CAMBRIDGE UNIVERSITY PRESS
Cambridge, New York, Melbourne, Madrid, Cape Town, Singapore, São Paulo, Delhi

Cambridge University Press
The Edinburgh Building, Cambridge CB2 8RU, UK

www.cambridge.org
Information on this title: www.cambridge.org/9780521739290

First published 2009

Printed in the United Kingdom at the University Press, Cambridge

A catalogue record for this book is available from the British Library

ISBN 978-0-521-739290 Student's Book without answers

ISBN 978-0-521-739306 Student's Book with answers

ISBN 978-0-521-739313 Set of 2 Audio CDs

ISBN 978-0-521-739320 Self-study Pack

Contents

Thanks and acknowledgements

The authors and publishers acknowledge the following sources of copyright material and are grateful for the permissions granted. While every effort has been made, it has not always been possible to identify the sources of all the material used, or to trace all copyright holders. If any omissions are brought to our notice, we will be happy to include the appropriate acknowledgements on reprinting.

Tessa Lucas and the National Federation of Women's Institute for the adapted text on p. 10 'Drop me a line!' from 'Friendship by Post', *Home and Country Magazine*, February 1992. Reproduced by kind permission of Tessa Lucas and the National Federation of Women's Institute; The Random House Group and Houghton Mifflin Harcourt for the text on p. 30 'Miss Rita Cohen' from *American Pastoral* by Philip Roth. Copyright © 1997 Philip Roth. Published by Jonathan Cape. Reprinted by permission of the Random House Group Ltd and Houghton Mifflin Harcourt Publishing Company. All rights reserved; Telegraph Media Group Limited for the adapted text on p. 41 'Bigfoot' from *The Young Telegraph Supplement* 13 February 1999, for the adapted text on p. 76 'Keeping the holiday-makers happy' from 'No time to Shilley-Chalet' from *The Telegraph* 26 February 1993. Copyright © The Telegraph Media Group Limited; Sainsbury's Magazine for the adapted text on p. 54 'In Hot Water' by Mary Kemp from *Sainsbury's Magazine*, January 1996. Copyright © Sainsbury's Magazine and Mary Kemp 1996; Frances Rickford for the adapted text on p. 57 'Young Shoppers' from 'Going off their trolleys' *The Guardian* 21 September 1993. Reproduced by kind permission of Frances Rickford; The Bookseller for the text on p. 74 'Acting minus the drama' by Benedicte Page, *The Bookseller*. Reproduced by permission of The Bookseller. The piece first appeared in 1999.

Colour section

Alamy/Ace Stock Ltd C10 (t), C11 (tl), C15 (cl), Alamy/Aliki Sapountzi/Aliki Image Library C11 (br), Alamy/Archivberlin Fotoagentur GmbH C10 (c), Alamy/Aurora Open C2 (l), Alamy/Brownstock Inc C11 (bl), Alamy/Daniel Dempster C14 (b), Alamy/Daniel Teetor C3 (b), Alamy/James Frank C5 (t), Alamy/Phil Willis C8 (t), Alamy/Photofusion C10 (b), Alamy/Travelshots.com C4 (b); Anthony Blake Photo Library C14 (b); Corbis C13 (t), Corbis/Dave Bartruff C2 (cr), Corbis/Phil Schermister C2 (br), Corbis/Richard Oliver C1 (b); Getty Images C2 (tr), Getty Images/Paul Gilham C3 (c), Getty Images/Image Bank C14 (t), Getty Images/Johner Images C15 (tl), Getty Images/Lonely Planet C16 (t), Getty Images/Photodisc C13 (b), Getty Images/Stone C16 (b), Getty Images/Taxi C1 (t), Getty Images/Tetra Images C3 (t); Image State/John Davis C5 (b), Image State/Premium C15 (cr); Life File/Jan Suttle C11 (tr), Pictures Color Library C12 (t), Pictures Color Library C4 (t), Pictures Color Library/Photo Location Ltd C15 (b); Rex Features/John Harmah C8 (b), Rex Features/Sipa Press C9 (t,b), C12 (b).

Picture research by Alison Prior

Design concept by Peter Ducker

Cover design by David Lawton

The recordings which accompany this book were made at Studio AVP and dsound, London.

Introduction

This collection of four complete practice tests comprises papers from the University of Cambridge ESOL Examinations First Certificate in English (FCE) examination; students can practise these tests on their own or with the help of a teacher.

The FCE examination is part of a suite of general English examinations produced by Cambridge ESOL. This suite consists of five examinations that have similar characteristics but are designed for different levels of English language ability. Within the five levels, FCE is at Level B2 in the Council of Europe's *Common European Framework of Reference for Languages: Learning, teaching, assessment*. It has also been accredited by the Qualifications and Curriculum Authority in the UK as a Level 1 ESOL certificate in the National Qualifications Framework. The FCE examination is widely recognised in commerce and industry and in individual university faculties and other educational institutions.

Examination	Council of Europe Framework Level	UK National Qualifications Framework Level
CPE Certificate of Proficiency in English	C2	3
CAE Certificate in Advanced English	C1	2
FCE First Certificate in English	B2	1
PET Preliminary English Test	B1	Entry 3
KET Key English Test	A2	Entry 2

Further information

The information contained in this practice book is designed to be an overview of the exam. For a full description of all of the above exams, including information about task types, testing focus and preparation, please see the relevant handbooks which can be obtained from Cambridge ESOL at the address below or from the website at: www.CambridgeESOL.org

University of Cambridge ESOL Examinations
1 Hills Road
Cambridge CB1 2EU
United Kingdom

Telephone: +44 1223 553997
Fax: +44 1223 553621
e-mail: ESOLHelpdesk@ucles.org.uk

The structure of FCE: an overview

The FCE examination consists of five papers.

Paper 1   Reading   1 hour
This paper consists of **three parts**, each containing a text and some questions. Part 3 may
contain two or more shorter related texts. There are **30 questions** in total, including multiple-
choice, gapped-text and multiple-matching questions.

Paper 2   Writing   1 hour 20 minutes
This paper consists of **two parts** which carry equal marks. In Part 1, which is **compulsory**,
candidates have to write either a letter or an email of between 120 and 150 words. In Part 2,
there are four tasks from which candidates **choose one** to write about. The range of tasks from
which questions may be drawn includes an article, an essay, a letter, a report, a review and a
short story. The last question is based on the set books. These books remain on the list for two
years. Look on the website or contact the Cambridge ESOL Local Secretary in your area for
the up-to-date list of set books. The question on the set books has two options, from which
candidates **choose one** to write about. In this part, candidates have to write between 120 and
180 words.

Paper 3   Use of English   45 minutes
This paper consists of **four parts** and tests control of English grammar and vocabulary. There
are **42 questions** in total. The tasks include gap-filling exercises, word formation and sentence
transformation.

Paper 4   Listening   40 minutes (approximately)
This paper consists of **four parts**. Each part contains a recorded text or texts and some
questions, including multiple-choice, sentence completion and multiple-matching. Each text is
heard twice. There is a total of **30 questions**.

Paper 5   Speaking   14 minutes
This paper consists of **four parts**. The standard test format is two candidates and two examiners.
One examiner takes part in the conversation while the other examiner listens. Both examiners
give marks. Candidates will be given photographs and other visual and written material to look
at and talk about. Sometimes candidates will talk with the other candidate, sometimes with the
examiner, and sometimes with both.

Grading

The overall FCE grade is based on the total score gained in all five papers. Each paper is
weighted to 40 marks. Therefore, the five FCE papers total 200 marks after weighting. It is not
necessary to achieve a satisfactory level in all five papers in order to pass the examination.
Certificates are given to candidates who pass the examination with grade A, B or C. A is the
highest. D and E are failing grades. All candidates are sent a Statement of Results which
includes a graphical profile of their performance in each paper and shows their relative
performance in each one.

For further information on grading and results, go to the website (see page 5).

Test 1

PAPER 1　READING (1 hour)

Part 1

You are going to read a magazine article about an artist who paints flowers. For questions **1–8**, choose the answer (**A**, **B**, **C** or **D**) which you think fits best according to the text.

Mark your answers **on the separate answer sheet.**

An eye for detail

Artist Susan Shepherd is best known for her flower paintings, and the large garden that surrounds her house is the source of many of her subjects. It is full of her favourite flowers, most especially varieties of tulips and poppies. Some of the plants are unruly and seed themselves all over the garden. There is a harmony of colour, shape and structure in the two long flower borders that line the paved path which crosses the garden from east to west.
line 12　Much of this is due to the previous owners who were keen gardeners, and who left plants that appealed to Susan. She also inherited the gardener, Danny. 'In fact, it was really his garden,' she says. 'We got on very well. At first he would say, "Oh, it's not worth it" to some of the things I wanted to put in, but when I said I wanted to paint them, he recognised what I had in mind.'

Susan prefers to focus on detailed studies of individual plants rather than on the garden as a whole, though she will occasionally paint a group of plants where they are. More usually, she picks them and then takes them up to her studio. 'I don't set the whole thing up at once,' she says. 'I take one flower out and paint it, which might take a few days, and then I bring in another one and build up the painting that way. Sometimes it takes a couple of years to finish.'

Her busiest time of year is spring and early summer, when the tulips are out, followed by the poppies. 'They all come out together, and you're so busy,' she says. But the gradual decaying process is also part of the fascination for her. With

tulips, for example, 'you bring them in and put them in water, then leave them for perhaps a day and they each form themselves into different shapes. They open out and are fantastic. When you first put them in a vase, you think they are boring, but they change all the time with twists and turns.'

Susan has always been interested in plants: 'I did botany at school and used to collect wild flowers from all around the countryside,' she says. 'I wasn't particularly interested in gardening then; in fact, I didn't like garden flowers, I thought they looked like the ones made of silk or plastic that were sold in some florists' shops – to me, the only real ones were wild. I was intrigued by the way they managed to flower in really awkward places, like cracks in rocks or on cliff tops.' Nowadays, the garden owes much to plants that originated in far-off lands, though they seem as much at home in her garden as they did in China or the Himalayas. She has a come-what-may attitude to the garden, rather like an affectionate aunt who is quite happy for children to run about undisciplined as long as they don't do any serious damage.

With two forthcoming exhibitions to prepare for, and a ready supply of subject material at her back door, finding time to work in the garden has been difficult recently. She now employs an extra gardener but, despite the need to paint, she knows that, to maintain her connection with her subject matter, 'you have to get your hands dirty'.

1 In the first paragraph, the writer describes Susan's garden as

   A having caused problems for the previous owners.
   B having a path lined with flowers.
   C needing a lot of work to keep it looking attractive.
   D being only partly finished.

2 What does 'this' in line 12 refer to?

   A the position of the path
   B the number of wild plants
   C the position of the garden
   D the harmony of the planting

3 What does Susan say about Danny?

   A He felt she was interfering in his work.
   B He immediately understood her feelings.
   C He was recommended by the previous owners.
   D He was slow to see the point of some of her ideas.

4 What is Susan's approach to painting?

   A She will wait until a flower is ready to be picked before painting it.
   B She likes to do research on a plant before she paints it.
   C She spends all day painting an individual flower.
   D She creates her paintings in several stages.

5 Susan thinks that tulips

   A are more colourful and better shaped than other flowers.
   B are not easy to paint because they change so quickly.
   C look best some time after they have been cut.
   D should be kept in the house for as long as possible.

6 Why did Susan enjoy studying wild flowers at school?

   A She found the way they adapted to their surroundings fascinating.
   B She used the lessons as a good excuse to get out of school.
   C She was attracted by their different colours and shapes.
   D She wanted to learn how to make copies of them in material.

7 How does the writer describe Susan's attitude to her garden?

   A She thinks children should be allowed to enjoy it.
   B She prefers planting flowers from overseas.
   C She likes a certain amount of disorder.
   D She dislikes criticism of her planting methods.

8 What point is Susan making in the final paragraph?

   A It's essential to find the time to paint even if there is gardening to be done.
   B It's important not to leave the gardening entirely to other people.
   C It's good to have expert help when you grow plants.
   D It's hard to do exhibitions if there are not enough plants ready in the garden.

Part 2

You are going to read a magazine article about letter writing. Seven sentences have been removed from the article. Choose from the sentences **A–H** the one which fits each gap (**9–15**). There is one extra sentence which you do not need to use.

Mark your answers **on the separate answer sheet**.

Drop me a line!

In our fast world of phones, emails and computers, the old-fashioned art of letter writing is at risk of disappearing altogether. Yet, to me, there is something about receiving a letter that cannot be matched by any other form of communication. There is the excitement of its arrival, the pleasure of seeing who it is from and, finally, the enjoyment of the contents.

Letter writing has been part of my life for as long as I can remember. It probably began with the little notes I would write to my mother. My mother, also, always insisted I write my own thank-you letters for Christmas and birthday presents. **9**

When I left home at 18 to train as a doctor in London, I would write once a week, and so would my mother. Occasionally my father would write and it was always a joy to receive his long, amusing letters. **10** Of course, we also made phone calls but it is the letters I remember most.

There were also letters from my boyfriends. In my youth I seemed to attract people who had to work or study away at some time and I was only able to stay in touch by correspondence. **11** I found that I could often express myself more easily in writing than by talking.

I love the letters that come with birthday or Christmas cards. **12** And it's even nicer

when it's an airmail envelope with beautiful stamps. My overseas letters arrive from Mangala in Sri Lanka, from someone I trained with over 20 years ago, and I have a penfriend in Australia and another in Vancouver.

Then there's the lady who writes to me from France. If we hadn't started talking in a restaurant on the way home from holiday, if my husband hadn't taken her photo and if I hadn't asked her for her address, I would never have been able to write to her. **13** As it is, we now have a regular correspondence. I can improve my French (she speaks no English); we have stayed at her home twice and she has stayed with us.

My biggest letter-writing success, however, came this summer, when my family and I stayed with my American penfriend in Texas. **14** Everyone was amazed that a correspondence could last so long. The local press even considered the correspondence worth reporting on the front page.

I am pleased that my children are carrying on the tradition. Like my mother before me, I insist they write their own thank-you letters. My daughter writes me little letters, just as I did to my mother. **15** However convenient communicating by email may appear to be, I strongly urge readers not to allow letter writing to become another 'lost art'.

A Most of the letters from home contained just everyday events concerning my parents and their friends.

B We had been corresponding for 29 years but had never met.

C It didn't matter how short or untidy they were as long as they were letters.

D Notes are appreciated, but how much better to have a year's supply of news!

E Poor handwriting can spoil your enjoyment of a letter.

F But instead of harming the relationships, letter writing seemed to improve them.

G She and my son have penfriends of their own in Texas, organised by my penfriend.

H More important, if she hadn't replied, we would be the poorer for it.

Part 3

You are going to read a magazine article in which five people talk about railway journeys. For questions **16–30**, choose from the people (**A–E**). The people may be chosen more than once. When more than one answer is required, these may be given in any order.

Mark your answers **on the separate answer sheet**.

Which person or people

found on returning years later that nothing had changed?	**16**
was unsure of the number of passengers on the train?	**17**
enjoyed the company of fellow passengers?	**18**
found the views from the train dramatic?	**19** **20**
welcomed a chance to relax on the trip?	**21**
was never disappointed by the journey?	**22**
has a reason for feeling grateful to one special train?	**23**
travelled on a railway which is no longer in regular service?	**24**
regretted not going on a particular train trip?	**25**
used to travel on the railway whenever possible?	**26**
learnt an interesting piece of information on a train journey?	**27**
took a train which travelled from one country to another?	**28**
says that the railway had been looked after by unpaid helpers?	**29**
was once considered not old enough to travel by train?	**30**

On the rails

Five celebrities tell Andrew Morgan their favourite memories of railway journeys.

| A | Andrea Thompson – Newsreader |

I fell in love with the south of France a long time ago and try to get back there as often as I can. There's a local train from Cannes along the coast which crosses the border with Italy. It takes you past some of the most amazing seascapes. It never matters what the weather is like, or what time of the year it is, it is always enchanting. Out of the other window are some of the best back gardens and residences in the whole of France. You feel like someone peeping into the property of the rich and famous. The travellers themselves are always lively because there is an interesting mix of tourists and locals, all with different itineraries but all admirers of the breathtaking journey.

| B | Raj Patel – Explorer |

I have enjoyed so many rail journeys through the years, but if I had to pick a favourite it would be the Nile Valley Express, which runs across the desert of northern Sudan. The one misfortune in my youth, growing up in South Africa, was missing out on a family train journey from Cape Town to the Kruger National Park. I was regarded as being too young and troublesome and was sent off to an aunt. When I came to live in England as a teenager, I still hadn't travelled by train. London Waterloo was the first real station I ever saw and its great glass dome filled me with wonder.

| C | Betty Cooper – Novelist |

I am indebted to one train in particular: the Blue Train, which took my husband and me on our honeymoon across France to catch a boat to Egypt. It was on the train that my husband gave me a pink dress, which I thought was absolutely wonderful. Someone happened to mention that pink was good for the brain, and I've never stopped wearing the colour since. What I remember about the journey itself, however, is how lovely it was to travel through France and then by boat up the Nile to Luxor. It was, without a doubt, the perfect way to wind down after all the wedding preparations.

| D | Martin Brown – Journalist |

We were working on a series of articles based on a round-the-world trip and had to cross a desert in an African country. There wasn't a road, so the only way we could continue our journey was to take what was affectionately known as the Desert Express. The timetable was unreliable – we were just given a day. We also heard that, in any case, the driver would often wait for days to depart if he knew there were people still on their way. When it appeared, there was a sudden charge of what seemed like hundreds of people climbing into and onto the carriages – people were even allowed to travel on the roof free. During the night, the train crossed some of the most beautiful landscapes I have ever seen. It was like a dream, like travelling across the moon.

| E | Arisu Mezuki – Actress |

I imagine most people's favourite impressions of trains and railways are formed when they are young children, but that's not my case. I was brought up in Singapore and Cyprus, where I saw very few trains, let alone travelled on them. It wasn't until I was a teenager that trains began to dominate my life. I made a film which featured a railway in Yorkshire. Most of the filming took place on an old, disused stretch of the line which had been lovingly maintained by volunteers. That's where my passion for steam trains began. When we weren't filming, we took every opportunity to have a ride on the train, and, when I went back last year, it was as if time had stood still. Everything was still in place, even the gas lights on the station platform!

PAPER 2   WRITING (1 hour 20 minutes)

Part 1

You **must** answer this question. Write your answer in **120–150** words in an appropriate style.

---

1   Your English friend Bill is a travel writer. He has written a chapter for a guidebook about a town you know well and you have just read it. Read Bill's letter and your notes. Then write a letter to Bill using **all** your notes.

> *Thanks for agreeing to check the chapter that I've written. Could you let me know what you liked about it? Also, if any of the information is inaccurate, please give me the correct information! And do you think there's anything else I should include?*
>
> *Once again, thanks a lot for reading the chapter.*
>
> *Bill*

Notes for letter to Bill

- Tell Bill what I liked about his chapter –
  places to visit, ...

- Give Bill correct information about
  – parking in city centre
  – museum opening times

- Suggest Bill includes information about nightlife –
  give him details

Write your **letter**. You must use grammatically correct sentences with accurate spelling and punctuation in a style appropriate for the situation.

Do not write any postal addresses.

Part 2

Write an answer to **one** of the questions **2–5** in this part. Write your answer in **120–180** words in an appropriate style.

---

2   You recently saw this notice in an English language computer magazine.

> ### Reviews needed!
> Do you play computer games? Write us a review of a computer game that you enjoy.
> Describe the game's good and bad points and say how easy or difficult it is to play.
> Also say what age group it is suitable for.
>
> A free game for the best review!

Write your **review**.

3   Your teacher has asked you to write a story for the college English language magazine. The story must **begin** with the following words:

It was only a small mistake but it changed my life for ever.

Write your **story**.

4   You have seen the following notice in an international magazine.

> # COMPETITION
> **Is it better to live in a flat, a modern house or an old house?**
> **Write us an article giving your opinions.**
> **The best article will be published and the writer will receive £500.**

Write your **article**.

5   Answer **one** of the following two questions based on **one** of the titles below.

(a)   *Officially Dead* by Richard Prescott
      This is part of a letter from your friend Matthew.

> *In the book 'Officially Dead', Colin Fenton doesn't behave very well, does he? Do you have any sympathy for him or not?*
> *Write and tell me what you think. Matthew*

      Write your **letter** to Matthew. Do not write any postal addresses.

(b)   *Pride and Prejudice* by Jane Austen
      Your English teacher has given you this essay for homework.

      Compare the characters of Mr and Mrs Bennett and say whether you think they have a good marriage or not.

      Write your **essay**.

PAPER 3   USE OF ENGLISH (45 minutes)

Part 1

For questions **1–12**, read the text below and decide which answer (**A, B, C or D**) best fits each gap. There is an example at the beginning (**0**).

Mark your answers **on the separate answer sheet**.

Example:

0   A joined   **B** held   **C** were   **D** took

0	A	B	C	D
	—	—	—	▬

Thomas Edison

On the night of 21 October 1931, millions of Americans **(0)** ..... part in a coast-to-coast ceremony to commemorate the passing of a great man. Lights **(1)** ..... in homes and offices from New York to California. The ceremony **(2)** ..... the death of arguably the most important inventor of **(3)** ..... time: Thomas Alva Edison.

Few inventors have **(4)** ..... such an impact on everyday life, and many of his inventions played a crucial **(5)** ..... in the development of modern technology. One should never **(6)** ..... how revolutionary some of Edison's inventions were.

In many ways, Edison is the perfect example of an inventor – that is, not just someone who **(7)** ..... up clever gadgets, but someone whose products transform the lives of millions. He possessed the key characteristics that an inventor needs to **(8)** ..... a success of inventions, notably sheer determination. Edison famously tried thousands of materials while working on a new type of battery, reacting to failure by cheerfully **(9)** ..... to his colleagues: 'Well, **(10)** ..... we know 8,000 things that don't work.' Knowing when to take no **(11)** ..... of experts is also important. Edison's proposal for electric lighting circuitry was **(12)** ..... with total disbelief by eminent scientists, until he lit up whole streets with his lights.

1 **A** turned out   **B** came off   **C** went out   **D** put off

2 **A** marked   **B** distinguished   **C** noted   **D** indicated

3 **A** whole   **B** full   **C** entire   **D** all

4 **A** put   **B** had   **C** served   **D** set

5 **A** effect   **B** place   **C** role   **D** share

6 **A** underestimate   **B** lower   **C** decrease   **D** mislead

7 **A** creates   **B** shapes   **C** dreams   **D** forms

8 **A** gain   **B** make   **C** achieve   **D** get

9 **A** announcing   **B** informing   **C** instructing   **D** notifying

10 **A** by far   **B** at least   **C** even though   **D** for all

11 **A** notice   **B** regard   **C** attention   **D** view

12 **A** gathered   **B** caught   **C** drawn   **D** received

Part 2

For questions **13–24**, read the text below and think of the word which best fits each gap. Use only **one** word in each gap. There is an example at the beginning (**0**).

Write your answers **IN CAPITAL LETTERS on the separate answer sheet**.

Example: | 0 | A | F | T | E | R | | | | | | | | | | | | | |

Vancouver

Vancouver in western Canada is named (**0**) ..*after*.. Captain George Vancouver of the British

Royal Navy. However, Captain Vancouver was not the first European (**13**) ……….. visit the area –

the coast (**14**) ……….. already been explored by the Spanish. Nor did Captain Vancouver spend

many days there, even (**15**) ……….. the scenery amazed him and everyone else (**16**) ……….. was

travelling with him.

The scenery still amazes visitors to (**17**) ……….. city of Vancouver today. First-time visitors who

are (**18**) ……….. search of breathtaking views are usually directed to a beach about ten minutes

(**19**) ……….. the city centre. There, looking out over the sailing boats racing across the blue

water, visitors see Vancouver's towering skyline backed by the magnificent Coast Mountains.

The city is regularly picked by international travel associations (**20**) ……….. one of the world's

best tourist destinations. They are only confirming what the two million residents and eight

million tourists visiting Greater Vancouver (**21**) ……….. single year are always saying: there is

simply (**22**) ……….. other place on earth quite (**23**) ……….. it. It's not just the gorgeous setting

that appeals to people, (**24**) ……….. also Vancouver's wide range of sporting, cultural and

entertainment facilities.

Part 3

For questions **25–34**, read the text below. Use the word given in capitals at the end of some of the lines to form a word that fits in the gap **in the same line**. There is an example at the beginning (**0**).

Write your answers **IN CAPITAL LETTERS on the separate answer sheet**.

Example:

| 0 | A | M | A | Z | E | M | E | N | T | | | | | | | | |

A job with risks

Have you ever got really caught up in the excitement and emotion of a
good action film, and wondered in (**0**) .amazement. how film stars manage   **AMAZE**
to perform (**25**) .... acts like jumping off buildings or driving at great   **DANGER**
speed? Of course, it is only a momentary feeling as it is no secret that the
real (**26**) .... are almost invariably stunt men or women, who can earn   **PERFORM**
a very good (**27**) .... by standing in for the stars when necessary. The   **LIVE**
work is (**28**) .... demanding, and before qualifying for this job they have   **INCREDIBLE**
to undergo a rigorous training programme and (**29**) .... their ability in   **PROOF**
a number of sports including skiing, riding and gymnastics.

Naturally, the (**30**) .... of the stunt performer is of the utmost   **SAFE**
importance. Much depends on the performer getting the timing exactly
right so everything is planned down to the (**31**) .... detail. In a scene   **TINY**
which involves a complicated series of actions, there is no time for
(**32**) .... mistakes. A stunt man or woman often has only one chance   **CARE**
of getting things right, (**33**) .... film stars, who can, if necessary, film a   **LIKE**
scene (**34**) .... until it gains the director's approval.   **REPEAT**

Part 4

For questions **35–42**, complete the second sentence so that it has a similar meaning to the first sentence, using the word given. **Do not change the word given**. You must use between **two** and **five** words, including the word given.

Example:

0   A very friendly taxi driver drove us into town.

DRIVEN

We .... a very friendly taxi driver.

The gap can be filled by the words 'were driven into town by', so you write:

Example:	**0**	*WERE DRIVEN INTO TOWN BY*

Write **only** the missing words **IN CAPITAL LETTERS on the separate answer sheet**.

---

35   'Don't sit in front of the computer for too long,' our teacher told us.

WARNED

Our teacher .... in front of the computer for too long.

36   We got lost coming home from the leisure centre.

WAY

We couldn't .... from the leisure centre.

37   Mary didn't find it difficult to pass her driving test.

DIFFICULTY

Mary had .... her driving test.

38   I always trust Carla's advice.

SOMEBODY

Carla .... advice I always trust.

39 We appear to have been given the wrong address.

AS

It .... we have been given the wrong address.

40 I couldn't understand the instructions for my new DVD player.

SENSE

The instructions for my new DVD player didn't .... me.

41 It's a pity we didn't do more sport when I was at school.

COULD

I wish that .... more sport when I was at school.

42 He described the hotel to us in detail.

DETAILED

He .... of the hotel.

PAPER 4   LISTENING (approximately 40 minutes)

Part 1

You will hear people talking in eight different situations. For questions **1–8**, choose the best answer (**A**, **B** or **C**).

---

1   You overhear a young man talking about his first job.
How did he feel in his first job?

  A   bored

  B   confused

  C   enthusiastic

2   You hear a radio announcement about a dance company.
What are listeners being invited to?

  A   a show

  B   a talk

  C   a party

3   You overhear a woman talking to a man about something that happened to her.
Who was she?

  A   a pedestrian

  B   a driver

  C   a passenger

4   You hear a woman talking on the radio about her work making wildlife films.
What is her main point?

  A   Being in the right place at the right time is a matter of luck.

  B   More time is spent planning than actually filming.

  C   It is worthwhile spending time preparing.

5 You hear part of a travel programme on the radio.
Where is the speaker?

A outside a café

B by the sea

C on a lake

6 You overhear a woman talking about a table-tennis table in a sports shop.
What does she want the shop assistant to do about her table-tennis table?

A provide her with a new one

B have it put together for her

C give her the money back

7 You hear part of an interview with a businesswoman.
What is her business?

A hiring out boats

B hiring out caravans

C building boats

8 You hear a man talking on the radio.
Who is talking?

A an actor

B a journalist

C a theatre-goer

Part 2

You will hear a radio interview with Mike Reynolds, whose hobby is exploring underground places such as caves. For questions **9–18**, complete the sentences.

Cavers explore underground places such as mines and

| | **9** | as well as caves.

When cavers camp underground, they choose places which have

| *and* | **10** | available.

In the UK, the place Mike likes best for caving is | | **11**

As a physical activity, Mike compares caving to | | **12**

Cavers can pay as much as £20 for a suitable | | **13**

Cavers can pay as much as £50 for the right kind of

| | **14** |, which is worn on the head.

Mike recommends buying expensive

| | **15** | to avoid having accidents.

Caving is a sport for people of | | **16** | and backgrounds.

Some caves in Britain are called 'places of | | **17**

The need for safety explains why people don't organise caving

| | **18**

Part 3

You will hear five different people talking about their work on a cruise ship. For questions **19–23**, choose from the list (**A–F**) what each speaker says about their work. Use the letters only once. There is one extra letter which you do not need to use.

A One aspect of my job is less interesting than others.

Speaker 1   [ ] **19**

B My job involves planning for the unexpected.

Speaker 2   [ ] **20**

C You have to be sociable to do my job.

Speaker 3   [ ] **21**

D I don't like routine in my working life.

Speaker 4   [ ] **22**

E There's not much work to do during the day.

Speaker 5   [ ] **23**

F I provide passengers with a souvenir of their trip.

Part 4

You will hear an interview with a man called Stan Leach who is talking about adventure sports. For questions **24–30**, choose the best answer (**A, B** or **C**).

24 Stan says that the best thing about walking is that you can

    A   get fit by doing it.

    B   please yourself how you do it.

    C   do it on your own.

25 Stan's opinion on scrambling is that

    A   people doing it may need to be accompanied.

    B   it is unsuitable for beginners.

    C   it is more exciting than walking.

26 What did Stan discover when he went climbing?

    A   It was not enjoyable.

    B   It was harder than he expected.

    C   It can be very frightening.

27 What does Stan say about mountain biking?

    A   Britain is not the best place for it.

    B   It is more expensive in Britain than elsewhere.

    C   It is best where there are lots of downhill slopes.

28 Stan's advice on scuba diving is that

    A   most of the courses for it are good.

    B   it is easier than it seems.

    C   you should think carefully before trying it.

29 What is Stan's view of skydiving?

    A It is surprisingly popular.

    B It is best when done in teams.

    C Only certain types of people like it.

30 What does Stan say about canoeing?

    A You can do it in conditions that suit you.

    B It is best at certain times of the year.

    C There are few places in Britain to do it.

PAPER 5   SPEAKING (14 minutes)

You take the Speaking test with another candidate, referred to here as your partner. There are two examiners. One will speak to you and your partner and the other will be listening. Both examiners will award marks.

Part 1 (3 minutes)

The examiner asks you and your partner questions about yourselves. You may be asked about things like 'your home town', 'your interests', 'your career plans', etc.

Part 2 (a one-minute 'long turn' for each candidate, plus 20-second response from the second candidate)

The examiner gives you two photographs and asks you to talk about them for one minute. The examiner then asks your partner a question about your photographs and your partner responds briefly.

Then the examiner gives your partner two different photographs. Your partner talks about these photographs for one minute. This time the examiner asks you a question about your partner's photographs and you respond briefly.

Part 3 (approximately 3 minutes)

The examiner asks you and your partner to talk together. You may be asked to solve a problem or try to come to a decision about something. For example, you might be asked to decide the best way to use some rooms in a language school. The examiner gives you a picture to help you but does not join in the conversation.

Part 4 (approximately 4 minutes)

The examiner asks some further questions, which leads to a more general discussion of what you have talked about in Part 3. You may comment on your partner's answers if you wish.

Test 2

PAPER 1   READING (1 hour)

Part 1

You are going to read an extract from a novel. For questions **1–8**, choose the answer (**A**, **B**, **C** or **D**) which you think fits best according to the text.

Mark your answers **on the separate answer sheet**.

Miss Rita Cohen, a tiny, pale-skinned girl who looked half the age of Seymour's daughter, Marie, but claimed to be some six years older, came to his factory one day. She was dressed in overalls and ugly big shoes, and a bush of wiry hair framed her pretty face. She was so tiny, so young that he could barely believe that she was at the University of Pennsylvania, doing research into the leather industry in New Jersey for her Master's degree.

Three or four times a year someone either phoned Seymour or wrote to him to ask permission to see his factory, and occasionally he would assist a student by answering questions over the phone or, if the student struck him as especially serious, by offering a brief tour.

Rita Cohen was nearly as small, he thought, as the children from Marie's third-year class, who'd been brought the 50 kilometres from their rural schoolhouse one day, all those years ago, so that Marie's daddy could show them how he made gloves, show them especially Marie's favourite spot, the laying-off table, where, at the end of the process, the men shaped and pressed each and every glove by pulling it carefully

line 13 down over steam-heated brass hands. The hands were dangerously hot and they were shiny and they stuck straight up from the table in a row, thin-looking, like hands that had been flattened. As a little girl, Marie was captivated by their strangeness and called them the 'pancake hands'.

He heard Rita asking, 'How many pieces come in a shipment?' 'How many? Between twenty and twenty-five thousand.' She continued taking notes as she asked, 'They come direct to your shipping department?'

He liked finding that she was interested in every last detail. 'They come to the tannery. The tannery is a contractor. We buy the material and they make it into the right kind of leather for us to work with. My grandfather and father worked in the tannery right here in town. So did I, for six months, when I started working in the business. Ever been inside a tannery?' 'Not yet.' 'Well, you've got to go to a tannery if

line 23 you're going to write about leather. I'll set that up for you if you'd like. They're primitive places. The technology has improved things, but what you'll see isn't that different from what you'd have seen hundreds of years ago. Awful work. It's said to be the oldest industry of which remains have been found anywhere. Six-thousand-year-old relics of tanning found somewhere – Turkey, I believe. The first clothing was just skins that were tanned by smoking them. I told you it was an interesting subject once you get into it. My father is the leather scholar; he's the one you should be talking to. Start my father off about gloves and he'll talk for two days. That's typical, by the way: glovemen love the trade and everything about it. Tell me, have you ever seen anything being manufactured, Miss Cohen?' 'I can't say I have.' 'Never seen anything made?' 'Saw my mother make a cake when I was a child.'

He laughed. She had made him laugh. An innocent with spirit, eager to learn. His daughter was easily 30 cm taller than Rita Cohen, fair where she was dark, but otherwise Rita Cohen had begun to remind him of Marie. The good-natured intelligence that would just waft out of her and into the house when she came home from school, full of what she'd learned in class. How she remembered everything. Everything neatly taken down in her notebook and memorised overnight.

'I'll tell you what we're going to do. We're going to bring you right through the whole process. Come on. We're going to make you a pair of gloves and you're going to watch them being made from start to finish. What size do you wear?'

1 What was Seymour's first impression of Rita Cohen?

    A She reminded him of his daughter.

    B She was rather unattractive.

    C She did not look like a research student.

    D She hadn't given much thought to her appearance.

2 Seymour would show students round his factory if

    A he thought they were genuinely interested.

    B they telephoned for permission.

    C they wrote him an interesting letter.

    D their questions were hard to answer by phone.

3 What did Seymour's daughter like most about visiting the factory?

    A watching her father make gloves

    B helping to shape the gloves

    C making gloves for her schoolfriends

    D seeing the brass hands

4 The word 'shiny' in line 13 describes

    A the look of the hands.

    B the size of the hands.

    C the feel of the hands.

    D the temperature of the hands.

5 What does 'that' in line 23 refer to?

    A the tannery business

    B a visit to a tannery

    C writing about leather

    D working with leather

6 Seymour says that most tanneries today

    A have been running for over a hundred years.

    B are located in very old buildings.

    C are dependent on older workers.

    D still use traditional methods.

7 What does Seymour admire about his father?

    A his educational background

    B his knowledge of history

    C his enthusiasm for the business

    D his skill as a glovemaker

8 When she was a schoolgirl, Marie

    A made her parents laugh.

    B was intelligent but lazy.

    C easily forgot what she had learned.

    D was hard-working and keen.

Part 2

You are going to read a newspaper article about human beings getting taller. Seven sentences have been removed from the article. Choose from the sentences **A–H** the one which fits each gap (**9–15**). There is one extra sentence which you do not need to use.

Mark your answers **on the separate answer sheet**.

It's true – we're all getting too big for our boots

Chris Greener was fourteen when he told his careers teacher he wanted to join the navy when he left school. 'What do you want to be?' asked the teacher. 'The flagpole on a ship?' The teacher had a point – because Chris, though still only fourteen, was already almost two metres tall. Today, at 228 cm, he is Britain's tallest man.

Every decade, the average height of people in Europe grows another centimetre. Every year, more and more truly big people are born. Intriguingly, this does not mean humanity is producing a new super race. **9** Only now are we losing the effects of generations of poor diet – with dramatic effects. 'We are only now beginning to fulfil our proper potential,' says palaeontologist Professor Chris Stringer. 'We are becoming Cro-Magnons again – the people who lived on this planet 40,000 years ago.'

For most of human history, our ancestors got their food from a wide variety of sources: women gathered herbs, fruits and berries, while men supplemented these with occasional kills of animals (a way of life still adopted by the world's few remaining tribes of hunter-gatherers). **10** Then about 9,000 years ago, agriculture was invented – with devastating consequences. Most of the planet's green places have been gradually taken over by farmers, with the result that just three carbohydrate-rich plants – wheat, rice and maize – provide more than half of the calories consumed by the human race today.

11 Over the centuries we have lived on soups, porridges and breads that have left us underfed and underdeveloped. In one study in Ohio, scientists discovered that when they began to grow corn, healthy hunter-gatherers were turned into sickly, underweight farmers. Tooth decay increased, as did diseases. Far from being one of the blessings of the New World, corn was a public health disaster, according to some anthropologists.

12 The fact that most people relying on this system are poorly nourished and stunted has only recently been tackled, even by the world's wealthier nations. Only in Europe, the US and Japan are diets again reflecting the richness of our ancestors' diets.

As a result, the average man in the US is now 179 cm, in Holland 180 cm, and in Japan 177 cm. It is a welcome trend, though not without its own problems. **13** A standard bed-length has remained at 190 cm since 1860. Even worse, leg-room in planes and trains seems to have shrunk rather than grown, while clothes manufacturers are constantly having to revise their range of products.

The question is: where will it all end? We cannot grow for ever. **14** But what is it? According to Robert Fogel, of Chicago University, it could be as much as 193 cm – and we are likely to reach it some time this century.

However, scientists add one note of qualification. Individuals may be growing taller because of improved nutrition, but as a species we are actually shrinking. During the last ice age, 10,000 years ago, members of the human race were slightly rounder and taller – an evolutionary response to the cold. (Large, round bodies are best at keeping in heat.) **15** And as the planet continues to heat up, we may shrink even further. In other words, the growth of human beings could be offset by global warming.

A We must have some programmed upper limit.

B As they benefit from the changes in agriculture, people expect to have this wide variety of foods available.

C In fact, we are returning to what we were like as cavemen.

D This poor diet has had a disastrous effect on human health and physique.

E Since the climate warmed, we appear to have got slightly thinner and smaller, even when properly fed.

F Nevertheless, from then on agriculture spread because a piece of farmed land could support ten times the number of people who had previously lived off it as hunter-gatherers.

G One research study found that they based their diet on 85 different wild plants, for example.

H Heights may have risen, but the world has not moved on, it seems.

Part 3

You are going to read an article about guidebooks to London. For questions **16–30**, choose from the guidebooks (**A–F**). The guidebooks may be chosen more than once. When more than one answer is required, these may be given in any order.

Mark your answers **on the separate answer sheet**.

Of which guidebook(s) is the following stated?

It is frequently revised.	**16**
It is quite expensive.	**17**
Its appearance is similar to other books by the same publisher.	**18**
It contains some errors.	**19**
It is reasonably priced.	**20**
It shows great enthusiasm for the city.	**21**
It has always been produced with a particular market in mind.	**22**
It is written by people who have all the latest information.	**23**
It is written in a friendly style.	**24** **25**
It is part of the first series of its kind to be published.	**26**
It omits some sights which should be included.	**27**
It contains more information than other guides.	**28**
It might appeal to London residents.	**29**
Its information about places to eat is enjoyable to read.	**30**

London Guidebooks

Visitors to London, which has so much to offer, need all the help they can get. Alastair Bickley takes his pick of the capital's guidebooks.

Guidebook A

Informal and familiar in tone, this valuable book has much to offer. Produced by the same people who put together London's principal listings magazine, this is right up to date with what's happening in the city – very much its home ground. It is concise enough to cater for those staying for just a couple of days, yet covers all areas of interest to visitors in an admirably condensed and approachable way. On balance, this is the single most handy book to have with you in London.

Guidebook B

This book is beautifully illustrated, with cutaway diagrams of buildings and bird's-eye-view itineraries rather than plain maps. This is a model of the clear, professional design that is the recognisable trademark of this series. Its coverage of the main sights is strong, and visually it's a real treat – a delight to own as a practical guide. It's a bit pricey but well worth a look when you visit the bookshop.

Guidebook C

Probably the best-suited for a longish stay in the city. This guide surpasses its competitors in its sheer depth of knowledge and in the detail it provides. It's particularly handy for the thorough stroller with plenty of time on his or her hands, covering virtually every building or monument of any interest – and with well-drawn maps of each area. Its coverage of all types of restaurants, which encourages you to go out and try them, can also be appreciated from the comfort of your armchair.

Guidebook D

It is astonishing – and perhaps the greatest tribute one can pay to London as a city – that it's possible to have a high-quality holiday there and scarcely spend anything on admission charges. In this guide, the obvious bargains (National Gallery, British Museum, etc.) are almost lost among an impressive range of places which cost nothing to visit. It should pay more attention to the numerous wonderful churches in the City of London but otherwise this is a must for the seriously budget-conscious or the Londoner who is looking for something different (like me). The book itself isn't quite free, but at £4.95 you have to admit it's not far off it.

Guidebook E

This is the latest in the longest-standing series of budget guides and, unlike its competitors, it is still definitely aimed at young backpackers. Its description of the sights is less detailed than most and the accuracy of some of the information is surprisingly poor for such a regularly updated publication. However, it manages to cram in everything of significance, and is strongly weighted towards practicalities and entertainment.

Guidebook F

Here is a guide which comes with a distinct personality rather than following the style of the series to which it belongs. It is chatty, companionable, opinionated, crammed full of history and anecdotes as well as practical information. I can best describe the experience (for that's what it is) of reading this book as follows: imagine arriving in town and being taken in hand by a local who is determined to show you the best of everything and to give you the benefit of their considerable experience of a city for which they obviously hold a passion. It's a real delight.

PAPER 2 WRITING (1 hour 20 minutes)

Part 1

You **must** answer this question. Write your answer in **120–150** words in an appropriate style.

---

1 Some British people are coming to your area and you have been asked to help organise the group's visit. Read the email you have received from Mrs Davidson, the leader of the group, and the notes you have made. Then write an email to Mrs Davidson using **all** your notes.

Email
From: Jane Davidson
Sent: 12 June
Subject: Group visit

Great! Festival on 5–6 July. Interesting because . . .

We plan to arrive on 2 July, and will leave on 7 July. Are these the best dates?

The group will be made up of 12 teenagers and 8 adults. I've been told the Grand Hotel is nice. Could you please tell me something about it?

Tell Mrs Davidson . . .

Some of the adults want to go shopping. Can you recommend one or two interesting shops to go to?

Suggest . . .

The teenagers would like to spend an afternoon playing sports. What are the main sports facilities in your area?

Explain to Mrs Davidson

We are all looking forward to our visit. Thank you very much for your help.

Jane Davidson

Write your **email**. You must use grammatically correct sentences with accurate spelling and punctuation in a style appropriate for the situation.

Part 2

Write an answer to **one** of the questions **2–5** in this part. Write your answer in **120–180** words in an appropriate style.

2   You have seen this announcement in an international music magazine.

MUSIC ON THE RADIO

Our readers tell us they love listening to music on the radio! What would your ideal evening music programme be? Write us an article:
● telling us what type of music you'd like to hear
● giving your suggestions for making the programme popular.
The writer with the best ideas will win £1,000.

Write your **article**.

3   You have had a class discussion on being rich and famous. Your teacher has now asked you to write an essay on the following statement:

Everybody would like to be rich and famous.

Write your **essay**.

4   This is part of a letter from an English friend, Jo.

I leave school this summer and have a year free before university. I want to come to your country. First I'd like to spend some time travelling. Then I'd like to find a job for three months. Please give me some advice on travelling and working in your country.

Thanks, Jo

Write your **letter** to Jo. Do not write any postal addresses.

5   Answer **one** of the following two questions based on **one** of the titles below.

(a) *Officially Dead* by Richard Prescott
     You receive this letter from your English friend Jaimie.

There are some very unpleasant characters in 'Officially Dead', aren't there? Which person do you dislike most and why? Write and tell me.
                                                                           Jaimie.

Write a **letter** to Jaimie.

(b) *Pride and Prejudice* by Jane Austen
     Your English teacher has given you this question for homework:

What future do you imagine for the marriages of the Wickhams and the Darcys?

Write your **essay**.

PAPER 3 USE OF ENGLISH (45 minutes)

Part 1

For questions **1–12**, read the text below and decide which answer (**A, B, C** or **D**) best fits each gap. There is an example at the beginning (**0**).

Mark your answers **on the separate answer sheet**.

Example:

0   A face   **B** outline   **C** surface   **D** top

0	A	B	C	D
	▄	▁	▁	▁

Under the city streets

While skyscraper offices and elegant apartment blocks remain the public **(0)** ..... of most major cities, these cities also have a mass of secret tunnels and hidden pipes below ground which keep everything working. This other world exists, forgotten or neglected by all but a tiny **(1)** ..... of engineers and historians.

For example, there are more than 150 kilometres of rivers under the streets of London. Most have been **(2)** ..... over and, sadly, all that **(3)** ..... is their names. Perhaps the greatest **(4)** ..... to the city is the River Fleet, a **(5)** ..... great river which previously had beautiful houses on its **(6)** .... It now goes underground in the north of the city and **(7)** ..... into the River Thames by Blackfriars Bridge.

The London Underground **(8)** ..... 1,000 kilometres of underground railway track winding under the capital and more than 100 stations below street level. Along some underground railway lines, commuters can sometimes catch a **(9)** ..... glimpse of the platforms of more than 40 closed stations which have been left under the city. **(10)** ..... some are used as film sets, most **(11)** ..... forgotten. Some have had their entrances on the street turned into restaurants and shops, but most entrances have been **(12)** ..... down.

1 **A** number   **B** amount   **C** total   **D** few

2 **A** covered   **B** protected   **C** hidden   **D** sheltered

3 **A** stays   **B** stops   **C** remains   **D** keeps

4 **A** miss   **B** absence   **C** waste   **D** loss

5 **A** once   **B** past   **C** then   **D** prior

6 **A** borders   **B** coasts   **C** banks   **D** rims

7 **A** gets   **B** flows   **C** leaks   **D** lets

8 **A** holds   **B** contains   **C** has   **D** consists

9 **A** rapid   **B** brief   **C** fast   **D** sharp

10 **A** Despite   **B** Unless   **C** Although   **D** Since

11 **A** lie   **B** last   **C** live   **D** lay

12 **A** pulled   **B** broken   **C** brought   **D** cut

Part 2

For questions **13–24**, read the text below and think of the word which best fits each gap. Use only **one** word in each gap. There is an example at the beginning (**0**).

Write your answers **IN CAPITAL LETTERS on the separate answer sheet**.

Example: | **0** | T | H | E | | | | | | | | | | | | | | | | |

My home town

I was born in one of (**0**) ....*the*.... most interesting cities in Malaysia. It has a rich, colourful history and many parts of the city have hardly changed at (**13**) .... during the last five centuries. However, nowadays, it is (**14**) .... longer the trade centre that it once (**15**) .... It is difficult to imagine that at one time its harbour (**16**) .... to be visited by over 2,000 ships a week, and that the huge warehouses along the quayside would have (**17**) .... full of spices and silks, jewels and tea.

The old city centre is small, which (**18**) .... it very easy to explore (**19**) .... foot. A river neatly divides the town, (**20**) .... only physically but in spirit too. On one side, you find many grand houses, but on crossing the river, you find yourself in ancient Chinatown, where you really (**21**) .... a step back into the past.

It is great fun to wander through the colourful, noisy backstreets. As (**22**) .... as having shops that sell a wide range of clothes and shoes, some of these streets are also famous (**23**) .... high-quality antiques. Unfortunately, most of the bargains disappeared many years ago. However, (**24**) .... you look around carefully, you can still come across an interesting souvenir.

Part 3

For questions **25–34**, read the text below. Use the word given in capitals at the end of some of the lines to form a word that fits in the gap **in the same line**. There is an example at the beginning (**0**).

Write your answers **IN CAPITAL LETTERS on the separate answer sheet**.

Example: | **0** | E | X | I | S | T | E | N | C | E | | | | | | | | |

Bigfoot

There are some people who believe in the (**0**) ...... *existence* ...... of Bigfoot, a   **EXIST**

(**25**) .... ape-like creature that is supposed to live in the mountains in   **MYSTERY**

the USA. In 1967 some hunters claimed to have (**26**) .... filmed such   **ACCIDENT**

a creature. The brief film, showing a huge creature walking slowly

through the undergrowth, was broadcast worldwide and caused quite a

sensation. Many people saw this as firm (**27**) .... that Bigfoot is real.   **PROVE**

But now researchers have come to the (**28**) .... that the film is merely a   **CONCLUDE**

trick. After conducting a close (**29**) .... of it, they claim to have   **ANALYSE**

identified a man-made fastener at the creature's waist. Bigfoot is,

therefore, (**30**) .... to be anything more than a very large man dressed   **LIKELY**

up in an animal suit.

Some Bigfoot fans remain unconvinced by the (**31**) .... , though. They   **SCIENCE**

claim it is extremely (**32**) .... that something as small as a zip fastener   **DOUBT**

could be reliably identified on such an old film. In (**33**) .... , they say   **ADD**

that the creature caught on camera does not move like a human and that

it is therefore (**34**) .... a wild creature of nature. The debate goes on.   **TRUE**

Part 4

For questions **35–42**, complete the second sentence so that it has a similar meaning to the first sentence, using the word given. **Do not change the word given**. You must use between **two** and **five** words, including the word given.

Example:

0   A very friendly taxi driver drove us into town.

DRIVEN

We .... a very friendly taxi driver.

The gap can be filled by the words 'were driven into town by', so you write:

Example:	0	*WERE DRIVEN INTO TOWN BY*

Write **only** the missing words **IN CAPITAL LETTERS on the separate answer sheet**.

---

35   The TV programme was so complicated that none of the children could understand it.

TOO

The TV programme was .... the children to understand.

36   Luke knocked over the old lady's bicycle by accident.

MEAN

Luke .... knock over the old lady's bicycle.

37   I've already planned my next holiday.

ARRANGEMENTS

I've already .... my next holiday.

38   They say the ice in Antarctica is getting thinner all the time.

SAID

The ice in Antarctica .... getting thinner all the time.

39 We didn't enjoy our walk along the seafront because it was so windy.

PREVENTED

The strong wind .... our walk along the seafront.

40 It looks as if Susan has left her jacket behind.

SEEMS

Susan .... her jacket behind.

41 A newly qualified dentist took out Mr Dupont's tooth.

HAD

Mr Dupont .... by a newly qualified dentist.

42 Antonio only lost the 100-metre race because he fell.

NOT

If Antonio had .... won the 100-metre race.

PAPER 4   LISTENING (approximately 40 minutes)

Part 1

You will hear people talking in eight different situations. For questions **1–8**, choose the best answer (**A, B** or **C**).

---

1   You hear part of an interview in which a film director talks about his favourite movie.
Why does he like the film?

   A   It is very funny.

   B   It is very exciting.

   C   It is very romantic.

2   You hear a man talking about a sofa he bought.
What is he complaining about?

   A   He received the wrong sofa.

   B   The shop overcharged him for the sofa.

   C   The sofa was damaged.

3   You hear an actor talking about using different accents in his work.
What point is he making about actors?

   A   They need to study a wide variety of accents.

   B   They have to be able to control their use of accents.

   C   They should try to keep their original accents.

4   You hear part of an interview in which a man is talking about winning his first horse race.
What does he say about it?

   A   He found it rather disappointing.

   B   He didn't have a chance to celebrate.

   C   He was too tired to care.

5 You hear a writer of musicals talking on the radio.
What is he trying to explain?

   A why his aunt's career was not very successful

   B the difference between American and British musicals

   C his reasons for becoming a writer of musicals

6 You hear the beginning of a lecture about ancient history.
What is the lecture going to be about?

   A trade in arms and weapons

   B trade in luxury household goods

   C trade in works of art

7 You hear a man talking about travelling from London to France for his job.
What does he say about the train journey?

   A He's able to use it to his advantage.

   B It's a boring but necessary part of his job.

   C He enjoys the social aspect of it.

8 You hear a woman in a shop talking about some lost photographs.
What does she think the shop should give her?

   A some money

   B a replacement film

   C an apology

Part 2

You will hear part of a radio interview with a woman who sailed round the world on her own. For questions **9–18**, complete the sentences.

Anna was employed by a [_____ **9**] when she first started sailing.

The idea of sailing round the world came from a book called

[_____ **10**]

Anna spent some time [_____ **11**] the boat before taking it out to sea.

Anna tested her boat on a trip which lasted for only

[_____ **12**] because it was damaged.

Anna got the money she needed to make the trip from various

[_____ **13**] companies.

Anna's worst problem during the trip was when she felt

[_____ **14**] because the boat was going so slowly.

Anna found the

[_____ **15**] in the Southern Ocean the most exciting part of the trip.

On her return, Anna phoned the [_____ **16**] to ask for a certificate.

Anna's claim was doubted because she hadn't been in contact with people on

[_____ **17**] during her trip.

Anna's story was finally believed after her

[_____ **18**] had been checked.

Part 3

You will hear five young people talking about what makes a good teacher. For questions **19–23**, choose from the list (**A–F**) which of the opinions each speaker expresses. Use the letters only once. There is one extra letter which you do not need to use.

A A good teacher praises effort.

	Speaker 1		19

B A good teacher knows the subject well.

	Speaker 2		20

C A good teacher is strict.

	Speaker 3		21

D A good teacher is available outside the classroom.

	Speaker 4		22

E A good teacher is entertaining.

	Speaker 5		23

F A good teacher has experience.

Part 4

You will hear a radio interview about a mountain-climbing weekend. For questions **24–30**, choose the best answer (**A**, **B** or **C**).

24 How did Douglas feel when he booked the weekend?

    A   sure that he would enjoy training for it

    B   uncertain if it was a good idea for him

    C   surprised that such activities were organised

25 Douglas expected that the experience would help him to

    A   meet people with similar interests.

    B   improve his physical fitness.

    C   discover his psychological limits.

26 He was surprised that the other participants

    A   were there for reasons like his.

    B   were experienced climbers.

    C   were in better condition than him.

27 What did one of his friends say to him?

    A   He was making a mistake.

    B   Climbing was fashionable.

    C   She was envious of him.

28 What did the people plan at the end of the trip?

    A   to send each other postcards

    B   to take a different sort of trip together

    C   to go on another climbing trip together

29 In what way did Douglas change as a result of the trip?

    A   He developed more interest in people.

    B   He became more ambitious.

    C   He began to notice more things around him.

30 Douglas's boots are still muddy because he wants them to

    A   remind him of what he has achieved.

    B   warn him not to do it again.

    C   show other people what he has done.

PAPER 5   SPEAKING (14 minutes)

You take the Speaking test with another candidate, referred to here as your partner. There are two examiners. One will speak to you and your partner and the other will be listening. Both examiners will award marks.

Part 1 (3 minutes)

The examiner asks you and your partner questions about yourselves. You may be asked about things like 'your home town', 'your interests', 'your career plans', etc.

Part 2 (a one-minute 'long turn' for each candidate, plus 20-second response from the second candidate)

The examiner gives you two photographs and asks you to talk about them for one minute. The examiner then asks your partner a question about your photographs and your partner responds briefly.

Then the examiner gives your partner two different photographs. Your partner talks about these photographs for one minute. This time the examiner asks you a question about your partner's photographs and you respond briefly.

Part 3 (approximately 3 minutes)

The examiner asks you and your partner to talk together. You may be asked to solve a problem or try to come to a decision about something. For example, you might be asked to decide the best way to use some rooms in a language school. The examiner gives you a picture to help you but does not join in the conversation.

Part 4 (approximately 4 minutes)

The examiner asks some further questions, which leads to a more general discussion of what you have talked about in Part 3. You may comment on your partner's answers if you wish.

Test 3

PAPER 1 READING (1 hour)

Part 1

You are going to read a magazine article in which a father describes his relationship with his son. For questions **1–8**, choose the answer (**A**, **B**, **C** or **D**) which you think fits best according to the text.

Mark your answers **on the separate answer sheet**.

Gary and Me

The restaurant owner John Moore writes about his relationship with his son Gary, the famous TV chef.

I believe everyone's given a chance in life. My son, Gary, was given his chance with cooking, and my chance was to run a restaurant. When I heard about the opportunity, I rushed over to look at the place. It was in a really bad state. It was perfect for what I had in mind.

Coming into this business made me recall my childhood. I can remember my mother going out to work in a factory and me being so upset because I was left alone. With that in mind, I thought, 'We want time for family life.' My wife dedicated herself to looking after the children and did all my accounts, while I ran the business. We lived over the restaurant in those days, and we always put a lot of emphasis on *line 16* having meals together. It's paid dividends with our children, Gary and Joe. They're both very confident. Also, from a very early age they would come down and talk to our regular customers. It's given both of them a great start in life.

Gary was quite a lively child when he was really small. We had a corner bath, and when he was about seven he thought he'd jump into it like a swimming pool, and he knocked himself out. When he was older he had to work for pocket money. He started off doing odd jobs and by the age of about ten he was in the kitchen every weekend, so he always had loads of money at school. He had discipline. He used to be up even before me in the morning. If you run a family business, it's for the family, and it was nice to see him helping out.

Gary wasn't very academic, but he shone so much in the kitchen. By the age of 15 he was as good as any of the men working there, and sometimes he was even left in charge. He would produce over a hundred meals, and from then I knew he'd go into catering because he had that flair. So when he came to me and said, 'Dad, I've got to do work experience as part of my course at school,' I sent him to a friend of mine who's got a restaurant.

Gary recently took up playing the drums and now he has his own band. Goodness knows what will happen to the cooking if the music takes off. My advice to Gary would be: if you start chasing two hares, you end up catching neither, so chase the hare you know you're going to catch. He understood when I said to him: 'Gary, if you're going to get anywhere in life, you've got to do it by the age of 30. If you haven't done it by then, it's too late.' *line 52*

Gary went to catering college at the age of 17, and on his first day he and the other new students – they're normally complete beginners – were given what's supposed to be a morning's work. But within an hour Gary had chopped all his vegetables, sliced all his meats. He'd prepared everything. That's my son for you! In the end, he was helping other people out.

None of us can believe how successful Gary's TV cookery series has become. I'm extremely proud of him. I've always tried to tell him that if you want something, you've got to work jolly hard for it, because no one gives you anything. He's seen the opportunity he's been given and grabbed hold of it with both hands. You know, you talk to your children as they grow up, and if they only take in ten per cent of what you've told them, you've got to be happy with that. The things Gary says, the things he does, I think, well, he must have listened sometimes.

1 How did the writer react to his own big chance?

    A He worried about the problems.
    B He saw what could be done.
    C He thought the family would suffer.
    D He wondered if he should take it.

2 How did the writer's childhood influence his own family life?

    A He realised that the pattern was repeating itself.
    B He encouraged his children to talk to him.
    C He made sure there was plenty of personal contact.
    D He asked his wife to stay at home.

3 What does the writer mean by 'paid dividends' in line 16?

    A brought financial reward
    B produced benefits
    C was worth the suffering
    D allowed money to be saved

4 As a young boy, Gary

    A showed how determined he could be.
    B was always in trouble.
    C was motivated by money.
    D demonstrated a variety of talents.

5 What is Gary's father's attitude to Gary playing in a band?

    A pleased that he has a hobby he enjoys
    B interested in how he can introduce music into the restaurant
    C concerned that music may interfere with his career
    D doubtful whether he will have time to improve his technique

6 What does 'done it' refer to in line 52?

    A chosen a profession
    B achieved success
    C caught a hare
    D lived your life

7 According to his father, what was typical about Gary's behaviour on his first day at college?

    A He helped other people.
    B He impressed those in charge.
    C He tried to make his father proud.
    D He performed the task efficiently.

8 How does his father regard Gary's upbringing?

    A His encouragement has caused Gary's success.
    B The family influence on Gary was too strong.
    C Gary has forgotten important lessons.
    D Gary has learnt some essential things.

Part 2

You are going to read an extract from a magazine article about underwater exploration. Seven sentences have been removed from the extract. Choose from the sentences **A–H** the one which fits each gap (**9–15**). There is one extra sentence which you do not need to use.

Mark your answers **on the separate answer sheet**.

IN HOT WATER

Rachel Mills is a scientist who spends as much time as she can at the bottom of the Atlantic Ocean.

Rachel Mills teaches and does research into marine geochemistry, which means she studies the chemical processes happening in the sea. She is a lecturer at the Oceanography Centre at Southampton University. When she isn't teaching, she lowers herself into a steel vehicle, a vessel for underwater exploration the size of a small car, and dives three kilometres down into the Atlantic Ocean to study underwater volcanoes.

'Inside,' she says, 'space is so limited that I can reach out and touch the two pilots.' **9** A dive can last for 16 hours – three hours to reach the ocean floor, ten hours gathering samples of rock and water and then three hours to get back up to the surface again.

'If anything happens, and you have a problem and have to get to the top quickly, you can hit a panic button.' The outside drops away leaving a small circular escape vessel that gets released, and it's like letting go of a ping-pong ball in the bath – it goes rapidly to the surface. **10**

'I didn't know how I was going to react the first time I climbed into the vehicle. It was on the deck of a ship and I got in with an instructor. **11** They were testing me to see how I would react to being in such a small place.'

Now Rachel has made six dives. Last year she dived with a Russian crew. 'We went to a site which was a five-day sail west of the Canary Islands in the Atlantic. **12** It is where the Atlantic Ocean comes alive. The Russian team were dropping off some scientific equipment there to discover the effect of a multi-national programme that would make a hole 150 metres through a volcano.'

When she isn't at sea, Rachel is in her office at the Oceanography Centre, Southampton. 'Two thirds of my salary comes from teaching, which I love, but I do it so I can get on with my research into the "black smokers".' This is just another name for underwater volcanoes – water comes out of the rock and turns into what looks like black smoke. **13**

'The only time I've been frightened is when I first went down with the Americans. We were towing equipment on a 50-metre rope when suddenly there was an explosion. There was this immense bang as the shock waves hit our vehicle and I thought, "I'm going to die." We stared at each other in silence, waiting. **14** The relief was incredible – we were still alive!'

'It's such an adventure diving down to the deepest part of the ocean. Every time I look out of the porthole and see those chimneys, there is such a sense of wonder. **15** I had studied the black smokers for three years for my PhD. When I got down there and saw them for real, it was such an amazing feeling.'

A Here, on the ocean floor, is a huge area of underwater volcanoes, their chimneys all blowing out black smoke.

B Here I am on the bottom of the sea, and no one else on this planet has ever before seen them.

C 'No one's tested it yet, but I don't think it would be a very pleasant journey.'

D He then talked me through the emergency procedures, including what to do if the pilot had a heart attack!

E They are used to these conditions, which mean they can't stand up or move, and they must stay inside until someone opens the door from the outside.

F When it didn't happen, we couldn't believe it.

G This pours out at a rate of one metre per second and at a temperature of 350 degrees.

H After that, as you get really deep, it's near freezing point so you need a sweater, thick socks, gloves and a woolly hat.

Part 3

You are going to read an article about the effect of advertising on children. For questions **16–30**, choose from the sections of the article (**A–F**). The sections may be chosen more than once.

Mark your answers **on the separate answer sheet**.

Which section of the article mentions

the kind of shop in which TV advertising expects to see results?	16
the influence a parent has had over their child's views?	17
the fact that children do not understand why their parents refuse their demands?	18
a parent who understands why children make demands?	19
a family who rarely argue while shopping?	20
someone who feels children ought to find out for themselves how to make decisions about what to buy?	21
the fact that parents can be mistaken about what food is good for you?	22
an unexpected benefit for shops?	23
a parent who regrets buying what their children have asked for?	24
a parent who has different rules for themselves and their children?	25
a parent who feels annoyed even before the children ask for anything?	26
the fact that parents blame the advertisers for the difficult situation they find themselves in?	27
the regularity of children's demands?	28
the need for parents to discuss food with their children?	29
a TV advertising rule which has little effect?	30

Young Shoppers

A Supermarket shopping with children, one mother says, is absolute murder: 'They want everything they see. If it's not the latest sugar-coated breakfast cereal, it's a Disney video or a comic. Usually all three. I can't afford all this stuff and, anyway, if I agree to their demands I feel I've been persuaded against my better judgement and I feel guilty about buying and feeding them rubbish. Yet I hate myself for saying no all the time, and I get cross and defensive in anticipation as we leave home. I do my best to avoid taking them shopping but then I worry that I'm not allowing them to have the experience they need in order to make their own choices. I can't win.'

B Research has found that children taken on a supermarket trip make a purchase request every two minutes. More than £150 million a year is now spent on advertising directly to children, most of it on television. That figure is likely to increase and it is in the supermarket aisles that the investment is most likely to be successful. For children, the reasons behind their parents' decisions about what they can and cannot afford are often unclear, and arguments about how bad sugar is for your teeth are unconvincing when compared with the attractive and emotionally persuasive advertising campaigns.

C According to Susan Dibb of the National Food Alliance, 'Most parents are concerned about what they give their children to eat and have ideas about what food is healthy – although those ideas are not always accurate. Obviously, such a dialogue between parents and children is a good thing, because if the only information children are getting about products is from TV advertising, they are getting a very one-sided view. Parents resent the fact that they are competing with the advertising industry and are forced into the position of repeatedly disappointing their children.' The Independent Television Commission, which regulates TV advertising, prohibits advertisers from telling children to ask their parents to buy products. But, as Dibb points out, 'The whole purpose of advertising is to persuade the viewer to buy something. So even if they cannot say, "Tell your mum to buy this product," the intended effect is precisely that.'

D A major source of stress for some parents shopping with children is the mental energy required to decide which demands should be agreed to and which should be refused. One mother says she has patience when it comes to discussing food with her children, but she still feels unhappy about the way she manages their shopping demands: 'My son does pay attention to advertisements but he is critical of them. We talk a lot about different products and spend time looking at labels. I've talked about it so much that I've brainwashed him into thinking all adverts are rubbish. We have very little conflict in the supermarket now because the children don't ask for things I won't want to buy.'

E Parents also admit they are inconsistent, even hypocritical, in their responses to their children's purchasing requests. Mike, father of a son of seven and a daughter of three, says, 'We refuse to buy him the sweets he wants on the grounds that it's bad for him while we are busy loading the trolley with double cream and chocolate for ourselves. It's enjoyable to buy nice things, and it's quite reasonable that children should want to share that, I suppose. But I still find myself being irritated by their demands. It partly depends on how I feel. If I'm feeling generous and things are going well in my life, I'm more likely to say yes. It's hard to be consistent.'

F Supermarkets themselves could do a lot more to ease parent–child conflict by removing sweets from checkout areas or even by providing supervised play areas. Although parents might spend less because their children are not with them, the thought of shopping without your six-year-old's demands would surely attract enough extra customers to more than make up the difference.

PAPER 2   WRITING (1 hour 20 minutes)

Part 1

You **must** answer this question. Write your answer in **120–150** words in an appropriate style.

---

1   Your English friend Tom came to visit you recently and he has just sent you an email and
some photographs. Read Tom's email and the notes you have made. Then write an email to
Tom using **all** your notes.

Email
From: Tom Smith
Sent: 6 March
Subject: Visit

Thanks for taking me to the airport. I hope your journey
home wasn't too long. ————————————————————

*Over 3 hours
because . . .*

I really enjoyed staying with you. Here are the photos I
took. Which one do you like best?

Tell Tom

When I got home, I realised I'd left my watch behind. It's
green and gold. You haven't found it, have you?

*Yes! Explain
where . . .*

I think we'll have a great time together when you come here
in September. We could either spend the whole time in my
family's flat in the city or stay on my uncle's farm in the
countryside. Which would you like to do?

*Say which
and why*

Write your **email**. You must use grammatically correct sentences with accurate spelling and
punctuation in a style appropriate for the situation.

Part 2

Write an answer to **one** of the questions **2–5** in this part. Write your answer in **120–180** words in an appropriate style.

2   Your teacher has asked you to write an essay giving your opinions on the following statement:

Your teenage years are the best years of your life!

Write your **essay**.

3   You see the following notice in an international magazine.

Be someone famous for a day

If you could change places for 24 hours with a famous person alive today, who would you choose, and why?

The best article will be published in our magazine next month.

Write your **article**.

4   You recently attended a music festival. When you visited the organiser's website afterwards, you saw they were asking for reviews of the event. You decide to write a review for the website. In your review say what kind of music you heard at the festival and whether you would recommend the festival to other people in future years.

Write your **review**.

5   Answer **one** of the following two questions based on **one** of the titles below.

(a) *Officially Dead* by Richard Prescott
This is part of a letter from your English friend Emily.

> *The characters in 'Officially Dead' seem to be either very weak or very strong. Which character do you think is the strongest and which one is the weakest? Write and tell me. Emily*

Write your **letter** to Emily.

(b) *Pride and Prejudice* by Jane Austen
Your English teacher has given you this question for homework:

Which part of 'Pride and Prejudice' do you think is the most interesting, and why?

Write your **essay**.

PAPER 3   USE OF ENGLISH (45 minutes)

Part 1

For questions **1–12**, read the text below and decide which answer (**A, B, C** or **D**) best fits each gap. There is an example at the beginning (**0**).

Mark your answers **on the separate answer sheet**.

Example:

0   **A** catch   **B** pick   **C** find   **D** gain

0	A	B	C	D
	—	_	_	_

A good start to a holiday

I had never been to Denmark before, and when I set out to **(0)** ..... the ferry in early May, I little **(1)** ..... that by the end of the trip I'd have made such lasting friendships.

I wanted to **(2)** ..... my time well, so I had planned a route which would **(3)** ..... several small islands and various parts of the countryside. I arrived at Esbjerg, a **(4)** ..... port for a cyclist's arrival, where tourist information can be obtained and money changed. A cycle track **(5)** ..... out of town and down to Ribe, where I spent my first night.

In my **(6)** ..... , a person travelling alone sometimes meets with unexpected hospitality, and this trip was no **(7)** ..... . In Ribe, I got into conversation with a cheerful man who turned **(8)** ..... to be the local baker. He insisted that I should **(9)** ..... his family for lunch, and, while we were eating, he contacted his daughter in Odense. Within minutes, he had **(10)** ..... for me to visit her and her family. Then I was **(11)** ..... on my way with a fresh loaf of bread to keep me **(12)** ..... , and the feeling that this would turn out to be a wonderful holiday.

1 **A** wondered   **B** suspected   **C** doubted   **D** judged

2 **A** take   **B** serve   **C** exercise   **D** use

3 **A** include   **B** contain   **C** enclose   **D** consist

4 **A** capable   **B** ready   **C** favourable   **D** convenient

5 **A** leads   **B** rides   **C** moves   **D** connects

6 **A** experience   **B** knowledge   **C** observation   **D** information

7 **A** difference   **B** change   **C** exception   **D** contrast

8 **A** up   **B** out   **C** in   **D** over

9 **A** greet   **B** see   **C** join   **D** approach

10 **A** arranged   **B** fixed   **C** settled   **D** ordered

11 **A** passed   **B** sent   **C** begun   **D** put

12 **A** doing   **B** making   **C** being   **D** going

Part 2

For questions **13–24**, read the text below and think of the word which best fits each gap. Use only **one** word in each gap. There is an example at the beginning (**0**).

Write your answers **IN CAPITAL LETTERS on the separate answer sheet**.

Example: | 0 | A | W | A | Y | | | | | | | | | | | | | |

Dealing with waste plastic

Every year people throw (**0**) ...*away*... millions of tonnes of plastic bottles, boxes and wrapping. These create huge mountains of waste that are extremely hard to get (**13**) .... of. Now a new recycling process promises to reduce this problem by turning old plastic (**14**) .... new.

Scientists have taken (**15**) .... long time to develop their ideas because waste plastic has always been a bigger problem (**16**) .... substances like waste paper. You can bury plastic, but it takes many years to break down. If you burn it, it just becomes another form of pollution. A (**17**) .... products, for example bottles, can be re-used, but it is expensive or difficult to do this (**18**) .... a lot of plastic products.

Now a group of companies has developed a new method (**19**) .... recycling that could save almost (**20**) .... plastic waste. Nearly every type of waste plastic can be used: it does (**21**) .... have to be sorted. In addition, labels and ink may be left (**22**) .... the products. Everything is simply mixed together (**23**) .... heated to more than 400 degrees centigrade (**24**) .... that it melts. It is then cooled, producing a waxy substance that can be used to make new plastic products, including computer hardware.

Part 3

For questions **25–34**, read the text below. Use the word given in capitals at the end of some of the lines to form a word that fits in the gap **in the same line**. There is an example at the beginning (**0**).

Write your answers **IN CAPITAL LETTERS on the separate answer sheet**.

Example:

| 0 | A | S | L | E | E | P | | | | | | | | | | | |

An unusual swimming club

While most sensible people are still fast (**0**) ....*asleep*......, members of a   **SLEEP**

special club in Britain (**25**) .... leave the warmth of their beds for an   **CHEER**

(**26**) .... swim in water with a temperature struggling to get beyond   **ENERGY**

seven degrees centigrade. This behaviour may seem rather odd to you –

indeed, it may sound like complete (**27**) .... – but these swimmers   **MAD**

firmly believe that it is (**28**) .... to take exercise in this way, even in   **HEALTH**

the depth of winter.

(**29**) .... of the club requires daily swimming outdoors in a nearby   **MEMBER**

lake. When members are asked why they do it, the common (**30**) ....   **RESPOND**

is that it makes them feel wonderful. The swimmers claim that

immersing their bodies (**31**) .... in very cold water eventually makes   **REGULAR**

them more resistant to illness, especially coughs and colds. And there is

certainly evidence to suggest that an (**32**) .... in blood circulation can   **IMPROVE**

be achieved. However, such behaviour may not be such a good idea for

people who are not used to large and sudden (**33**) .... in temperature.   **DIFFERENT**

For many people, swimming in icy water would actually be (**34**) ....   **HARM**

Part 4

For questions **35–42**, complete the second sentence so that it has a similar meaning to the first sentence, using the word given. **Do not change the word given**. You must use between **two** and **five** words, including the word given.

Example:

0   You must do exactly what the manager tells you.

CARRY

You must .... instructions exactly.

The gap can be filled by the words 'carry out the manager's', so you write:

Example: | **0** | *CARRY OUT THE MANAGER'S* |

Write **only** the missing words **IN CAPITAL LETTERS on the separate answer sheet**.

---

35   The teacher postponed the theatre trip until the summer term.

OFF

The theatre trip .... the teacher until the summer term.

36   'What is the width of this cupboard?' Rebecca asked her sister.

WIDE

Rebecca asked her sister .... was.

37   George spent ages tidying up his room.

TOOK

It .... up his room.

38   A famous architect designed Dr Schneider's house for her.

HAD

Dr Schneider .... a famous architect.

39 'Peter, you've eaten all the ice cream!' said his mother.

ACCUSED

Peter's mother .... all the ice cream.

40 Jim fell off his bike because he wasn't looking where he was going.

PAYING

If Jim .... to where he was going, he wouldn't have fallen off his bike.

41 We might not find it easy to book a seat at the last minute.

COULD

It .... us to book a seat at the last minute.

42 It was wrong of you to borrow my jacket without asking.

OUGHT

You .... before you borrowed my jacket.

PAPER 4   LISTENING (approximately 40 minutes)

Part 1

You will hear people talking in eight different situations. For questions **1–8**, choose the best answer (**A**, **B** or **C**).

---

1   You hear a man talking to a group of people who are going on an expedition into the rainforest.
What does he advise them against?

    A   sleeping in places where insects are found

    B   using substances which attract insects

    C   bathing in areas where insects are common

2   You overhear two people talking about a school football competition.
What did the woman think of the event?

    A   She didn't think anyone had enjoyed it.

    B   It managed to fulfil its aims.

    C   Not enough people had helped to set it up.

3   You hear a woman talking about her studies at the Beijing Opera School.
How did she feel when she first started her classes?

    A   worried about being much older than the other students

    B   disappointed because her dictionary was unhelpful

    C   annoyed by the lack of communication with her teacher

4   You hear a famous comedian talking on the radio about his early career.
Why is he telling this story?

    A   to show how lucky he was at the beginning

    B   to show the value of a good course

    C   to show that he has always been a good comedian

5   You hear someone talking on the phone.
   Who is she talking to?

   A   someone at her office

   B   someone at a travel information centre

   C   a family member

6   You hear a novelist talking about how she writes.
   How does she get her ideas for her novels?

   A   She bases her novels on personal experiences.

   B   Ideas come to her once she starts writing.

   C   She lets ideas develop gradually in her mind.

7   You hear a woman talking to a friend on the phone.
   What is she doing?

   A   refusing an invitation

   B   denying an accusation

   C   apologising for a mistake

8   You hear a radio announcement about a future programme.
   What kind of programme is it?

   A   a play about a child

   B   a reading from a children's book

   C   a holiday programme

Part 2

You will hear an interview with a man who enjoys flying in a small aircraft called a microlight. For questions **9–18**, complete the sentences.

Before his retirement, Brian worked as a pilot for a company called

| | **9** | for a long time.

Brian feels like a bird when flying his microlight because he doesn't have a

| | **10** | around him.

Brian disagrees with the suggestion that steering a microlight is like steering a

| | **11** |

Brian's record-breaking flight ended in | | **12** |

Brian organised his flight in advance to avoid needing other people as

| | **13** | on the way.

Brian's microlight was modified so that it could carry more

| | **14** | on board.

It took Brian | | **15** | to plan the record-breaking flight.

Brian feels that flying over miles and miles of

| | **16** | was the most dangerous part of the trip.

Brian describes his navigation system as both

| | **17** | and easy to use.

Brian says that his main problem on the flight was the fact that he became very

| | **18** |

Part 3

You will hear five different people talking about short courses they have attended. For questions **19–23**, choose from the list (**A–F**) what each speaker says about their course. Use the letters only once. There is one extra letter which you do not need to use.

A I was encouraged by the teachers to continue developing my skill.

Speaker 1   **19**

B I learnt something about the subject that I hadn't expected.

Speaker 2   **20**

C I preferred the social life to the course content.

Speaker 3   **21**

D I intend doing a similar course again.

Speaker 4   **22**

E I found out something about myself.

Speaker 5   **23**

F I thought the course was good value for money.

Part 4

You will hear part of a radio interview with Martin Middleton, who makes wildlife programmes for television. For questions **24–30**, choose the best answer (**A**, **B** or **C**).

24 What was the origin of Martin Middleton's love of travel?

    A   living abroad in the 1960s

    B   something he read as a child

    C   a television film about Africa

25 When he visited Borneo, Martin

    A   had no fixed expectations.

    B   made a programme about life on the river.

    C   became more interested in filming old buildings.

26 Since the early 1960s, wildlife filming has become

    A   more relaxed.

    B   more creative.

    C   more organised.

27 Looking back, Martin regards his experience on the iceberg as

    A   slightly ridiculous.

    B   extremely dangerous.

    C   strangely depressing.

28 When he takes a holiday, Martin prefers to

    A   relax by the sea.

    B   stay in comfortable surroundings.

    C   travel for a particular reason.

29 Martin thought that the holiday-makers he saw in the Dominican Republic were

    A   risking their health.

    B   wasting opportunities.

    C   lacking entertainment.

30 What is Martin's opinion of tourism?

    A   It should be discouraged.

    B   It can be a good thing.

    C   It is well managed.

PAPER 5   SPEAKING (14 minutes)

You take the Speaking test with another candidate, referred to here as your partner. There are two examiners. One will speak to you and your partner and the other will be listening. Both examiners will award marks.

Part 1 (3 minutes)

The examiner asks you and your partner questions about yourselves. You may be asked about things like 'your home town', 'your interests', 'your career plans', etc.

Part 2 (a one-minute 'long turn' for each candidate, plus 20-second response from the second candidate)

The examiner gives you two photographs and asks you to talk about them for one minute. The examiner then asks your partner a question about your photographs and your partner responds briefly.

Then the examiner gives your partner two different photographs. Your partner talks about these photographs for one minute. This time the examiner asks you a question about your partner's photographs and you respond briefly.

Part 3 (approximately 3 minutes)

The examiner asks you and your partner to talk together. You may be asked to solve a problem or try to come to a decision about something. For example, you might be asked to decide the best way to use some rooms in a language school. The examiner gives you a picture to help you but does not join in the conversation.

Part 4 (approximately 4 minutes)

The examiner asks some further questions, which leads to a more general discussion of what you have talked about in Part 3. You may comment on your partner's answers if you wish.

Visual materials for the Speaking test

- What is it like to work in places like these?

1A

1B

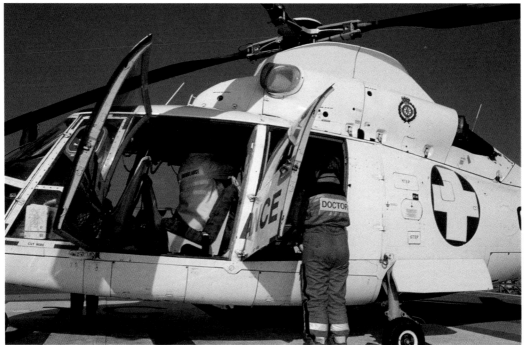

- Why do people choose to do these different kinds of sports?
- Which sport would be the most difficult to do well?

1E

- Why do people choose to go to places like these?

1C

1D

• What are the people feeling?

2A

2B

- What problems might your friend have?
- What could he or she do to avoid these problems?

2E

C7

- Why are the photographs being taken?

2C

2D

- What are the people feeling?

3A

3B

- What is good or bad about these people's jobs?
- Which three jobs would be most interesting to hear about?

3E

- What is enjoyable about music like this?

3C

3D

• Why are the people painting these walls?

4A

4B

- How important are these things for a happy life?
- Which two are the most important?

4E

• Why have the people chosen to go to these places?

4C

4D

Test 4

PAPER 1   READING (1 hour)

Part 1

You are going to read an article about the actress Harriet Walter. For questions **1–8**, choose the answer (**A, B, C** or **D**) which you think fits best according to the text.

Mark your answers **on the separate answer sheet**.

Acting minus the drama

Harriet Walter has written a fascinating book about her profession.
Benedicte Page reports.

It is not often that an experienced actor with a high public profile will sit down to answer in depth the ordinary theatregoer's questions: how do you put together a character which isn't your own?; what is it like to perform the same play night after night?; or simply, why do you do it? Harriet Walter was prompted to write *Other People's Shoes: Thoughts on Acting* by a sense that many people's interest in theatre extended beyond the scope of entertainment chit-chat. 'I was asked very intelligent, probing questions by people who weren't in the profession, from taxi drivers to dinner-party hosts to people in shopping queues. It made me realise that people have an interest in what we do which goes beyond show business gossip,' she says.

Other People's Shoes avoids insider gossip and, mostly, autobiography: 'If events in my life had had a huge direct influence, I would have put them in, but they didn't,' Harriet says, though she does explain how her parents' divorce was a factor in her career. But the focus of the book is to share – remarkably openly – the inside experience of the stage and the rehearsal room, aiming to replace the false sense of mystery with a more realistic understanding and respect for the profession.

'There's a certain double edge to the publicity an actor can get in the newspapers: it gives you attention but, by giving it to you, simultaneously criticises you,' Harriet says. 'People ask you to talk about yourself and then say, "Oh, actors are so self-centred." And the "sound-bite" variety of journalism, which touches on many things but never allows you to go into them in depth, leaves you with a sort of shorthand which reinforces prejudices and myths.'

Harriet's career began in the 1970s and has included theatre performances with the Royal Shakespeare Company and television and film roles. She writes wittily about the embarrassments of the rehearsal room, as actors try out their half-formed ideas. And she is at pains to demystify the theatre: the question 'How do you do the same play every night?' is answered by a simple comparison with the familiar car journey you take every day, which presents a slightly different challenge each time. 'I was trying to get everyone to understand it isn't this extraordinary mystery and you're not visited by some spiritual inspiration every night.'

line 50

Harriet's own acting style is to build up a character piece by piece. She says that this process is not widely understood: 'There's no intelligent vocabulary out there for discussing the craft of building characters. Reviews of an actor's performance which appear in the newspapers are generally based on whether the reviewer likes the actors or not. It's not about whether they are being skilful or not, or how intelligent their choices are.'

There remains something mysterious about slipping into 'other people's shoes': 'It's something like falling in love,' Harriet says. 'When you're in love with someone, you go in and out of separateness and togetherness. It's similar with acting and you can slip in and out of a character. Once a character has been built, it remains with you, at the end of a phone line, as it were, waiting for your call.'

Harriet includes her early work in *Other People's Shoes* – 'I wanted to separate myself from those who say, "What an idiot I was, what a load of nonsense we all talked in those days!"; it wasn't all rubbish, and it has affected how I approach my work and my audiences.' And she retains from those days her belief in the vital role of the theatre.

1   Harriet Walter decided to write her book because she

    A was tired of answering people's questions about acting.
    B knew people liked to read about show business gossip.
    C wanted to entertain people through her writing.
    D wanted to satisfy people's curiosity about acting in the theatre.

2   In paragraph two, we learn that Harriet's book aims to

    A correct some of the impressions people have of the theatre.
    B relate important details about her own life story.
    C analyse the difficulties of a career in the theatre.
    D tell the truth about some of the actors she has worked with.

3   What problem do actors have with newspaper publicity?

    A It never focuses on the actors who deserve it.
    B It often does more harm than good.
    C It never reports what actors have actually said.
    D It often makes mistakes when reporting facts.

4   Harriet uses the example of the car journey to show that

    A acting can be boring as well as rewarding.
    B actors do not find it easy to try new ideas.
    C actors do not deserve the praise they receive.
    D acting shares characteristics with other repetitive activities.

5   What does 'it' refer to in line 50?

    A facing a different challenge
    B taking a familiar car journey
    C acting in the same play every night
    D working with fellow actors

6   Harriet criticises theatre reviewers because they

    A do not give enough recognition to the art of character acting.
    B do not realise that some parts are more difficult to act than others.
    C choose the wrong kinds of plays to review.
    D suggest that certain actors have an easy job.

7   Harriet says that after actors have played a particular character, they

    A may be asked to play other similar characters.
    B may become a bit like the character.
    C will never want to play the part again.
    D will never forget how to play the part.

8   What does Harriet say about her early work?

    A It has been a valuable influence on the work she has done since.
    B It was completely different from the kind of work she does now.
    C She finds it embarrassing to recall that period of her life.
    D She is annoyed when people criticise the work she did then.

Part 2

You are going to read a magazine article about a girl and the job she does. Seven sentences have been removed from the article. Choose from the sentences **A–H** the one which fits each gap (**9–15**). There is one extra sentence which you do not need to use.

Mark your answers **on the separate answer sheet**.

Keeping the holiday-makers happy

A chalet girl's work is never done, Sarah Sutherland-Pilch tells Veronica Lee – in between making beds and delicious dinners.

This is the second year as a chalet girl for Sarah Sutherland-Pilch, a 24-year-old from West Sussex. Known by her nickname, Pilch, Sarah works for a company in Val d'Isère, France, cooking and cleaning for visitors who come to ski and stay in the wooden houses, known as chalets, that are characteristic of the area. Sarah graduated in French and History of Art from Oxford Brookes University last summer. Being a chalet girl isn't a career, she says, but an enjoyable way to spend a year or two before settling down. 'It's a good way to make contacts. I meet successful people every week.'

Sarah does not 'live in'. [__9__] She has her own breakfast before preparing that of the guests. 'They get the works – porridge, eggs, cereals, fruit and croissants.' When the last of the guests has had breakfast, by about 9.30 a.m., Sarah clears up and either makes the afternoon tea, which is left for the guests to help themselves to, or cleans the rooms – 'the worst part of the job,' she says.

By about 11 a.m. she is ready to go on the slopes herself. She skis as much as possible. [__10__] Sarah returns to the chalet in time to prepare dinner and takes a shower before doing so, but does not sleep. 'It's fatal if you do,' she says.

Dinner, a three-course affair, is served at 8 p.m. and coffee is usually on the table by 10 p.m. Sarah clears away the dinner things and fills the dishwasher. [__11__] Sometimes she will stay and chat with the guests, other times they are content to be left alone. 'Good guests can make a week brilliant – breakfast this morning was great fun – but some weeks, for whatever reason, don't go quite so well.'

Sarah meets her friends in the chalet where she lives – and they go out at about 11 p.m. 'We usually start off in *Bananas*, might go to *G Jay's* and perhaps *Dick's T-Bar* at the end of the evening,' she says. But Sarah never stays out too late on Saturday night as Sunday is her busiest time of the week. [__12__]

Work begins earlier than usual on Sunday, since breakfast for guests who are leaving has to be on the table by 7 a.m. [__13__] 'We just blitz the place – clear the breakfast, strip the beds, get everything ready.' If she hasn't already done the week's shop on Saturday, Sarah does it now.

[__14__] 'They get here at around 4.30 p.m. Sometimes they are disorientated and full of questions. I'm sure it's the mountain air that does something to them.'

Between tea and dinner, Sarah takes any guests needing boots or skis down to the ski shop and then gets a lift back to the chalet from one of the ski shop staff. [__15__] 'Sometimes I'm so tired I just have an early night,' she says.

A At around 3 p.m., the cleaning work done, Sarah then prepares tea for the new guests.

B Sarah enjoys cooking and, after leaving school, supported herself during holidays by working as a cook.

C 'There's nothing worse than coming in to a messy kitchen the next morning.'

D As soon as the guests are gone, Sarah starts cleaning madly.

E 'On a good day we can be up there until 4.30 p.m.'

F 'A frightful day,' she says, 'when you certainly don't want to be cooking breakfast feeling exhausted.'

G She gets up at 7 a.m. to walk the mile or so to the chalet, which sleeps up to 18 guests each week.

H It is soon time for dinner duty again and perhaps a chat with friends, but not always.

Part 3

You are going to read an article about people who changed their jobs. For questions **16–30**, choose from the people (**A–D**). The people may be chosen more than once.

Mark your answers **on the separate answer sheet.**

Which person mentions

enjoying their pastime more than the job they used to do?	**16**
enjoying being in charge of their own life?	**17**
being surprised by suddenly losing their previous job?	**18**
not having other people depending on them financially?	**19**
missing working with other people?	**20**
undergoing training in order to take up their new job?	**21**
a contact being useful in promoting their new business?	**22**
not being interested in possible promotion in their old job?	**23**
disliking the amount of time they used to have to work?	**24**
surprising someone else by the decision they made?	**25**
a prediction that hasn't come true?	**26**
consulting other people about their businesses?	**27**
the similarities between their new job and their old one?	**28**
working to a strict timetable?	**29**
needing time to choose a new career?	**30**

A NEW LIFE

A   The Farmer

Matt Froggatt used to be an insurance agent in the City of London but now runs a sheep farm.

'After 14 years in business, I found that the City had gone from a place which was exciting to work in to a grind – no one was having fun any more. But I hadn't planned to leave for another five or ten years when I was made redundant. It came out of the blue. I didn't get a particularly good pay-off but it was enough to set up the farm with. My break came when I got to know the head chef of a local hotel with one of the top 20 hotel restaurants in the country. Through supplying them, my reputation spread and now I also supply meat through mail order. I'm glad I'm no longer stuck in the office but it's astonishing how little things have changed for me: the same 80- to 90-hour week and still selling a product.'

B   The Painter

Ron Ablewhite was a manager in advertising but now makes a living as an artist.

'My painting began as a hobby but I realised I was getting far more excitement out of it than out of working. The decision to take redundancy and to become an artist seemed logical. The career counsellor I talked to was very helpful. I think I was the first person who had ever told him, "I don't want to go back to where I've been." He was astonished because the majority of people in their mid-forties need to get back to work immediately – they need the money. But we had married young and our children didn't need our support. It was a leap into the unknown. We went to the north of England, where we didn't know a soul. It meant leaving all our friends, but we've been lucky in that our friendships have survived the distance – plenty of them come up and visit us now.'

C   The Hatmaker

After working for five years as a company lawyer, Katherine Goodison set up her own business in her London flat, making hats for private clients.

'My job as a lawyer was fun. It was stimulating and I earned a lot of money, but the hours were terrible. I realised I didn't want to become a senior partner in the company, working more and more hours, so I left. A lot of people said I'd get bored, but that has never happened. The secret is to have deadlines. Since it's a fashion-related business, you have the collections, next year's shapes, the season – there's always too much to do, so you have to run a very regimented diary. I feel happier now, and definitely less stressed. There are things I really long for, though, like the social interaction with colleagues. What I love about this job is that I'm totally responsible for the product. If I do a rubbish job, then I'm the one who takes the blame. Of course, you care when you're working for a company, but when your name is all over the promotional material, you care that little bit more.'

D   The Masseur

Paul Drinkwater worked in finance for 16 years before becoming a masseur at the Life Centre in London.

'I had been in financial markets from the age of 22, setting up deals. I liked the adrenaline but I never found the work rewarding. I was nearly made redundant in 1989, but I escaped by resigning and travelling for a year. I spent that year trying to work out what I wanted to do. I was interested in health, so I visited some of the world's best gymnasiums and talked to the owners about how they started up. I knew that to change career I had to get qualifications so I did various courses in massage. Then I was offered part-time work at the Life Centre. I have no regrets. I never used to feel in control, but now I have peace of mind and control of my destiny. That's best of all.'

PAPER 2   WRITING (1 hour 20 minutes)

Part 1

You **must** answer this question. Write your answer in **120–150** words in an appropriate style.

---

1   You have just received an email from your English friend Alex asking if you'd like to go to a
    concert by your favourite band, Red Stone. Read Alex's email and the notes you have made.
    Then write an email to Alex using **all** your notes.

Email
From: Alex Gilbert
Sent: 6 May
Subject: Red Stone Concert

Guess what? Red Stone are giving a concert at the City
Stadium on Saturday 21 July. What about us going to see ——— *Yes!*
them together? I know you're a great fan of theirs, but I
don't really know anything about them.

Tell Alex
about the
I can get tickets if I book them this week. The ticket price   *band*
depends on whether we sit or stand – could you let me
know which you would prefer?

Say which
and why   You could stay the night with my family so we could do
something together the next day. Is there anything special
you'd like to do?

What about . . .?

Alex

Write your **email**. You must use grammatically correct sentences with accurate spelling and
punctuation in a style appropriate for the situation.

Part 2

Write an answer to **one** of the questions **2–5** in this part. Write your answer in **120–180** words in an appropriate style.

---

2   Your teacher has asked you for a report on transport in your local area. Mention the main means of transport used and suggest how transport facilities could be improved.

Write your **report**.

3   You see this notice on your school noticeboard.

> # SPECIAL PEOPLE
>
> - Who is the most important person in your life?
>
> - Why is this person special to you?
>
> Write us an article for the school magazine answering these questions.

Write your **article**.

4   Your teacher has asked you to write a story for the school's English language magazine. The story must **begin** with the following words:

My day started badly, but it got better and better.

Write your **story**.

5   Answer **one** of the following two questions based on **one** of the titles below.

  (a) *Officially Dead* by Richard Prescott
     You have discussed the character of Julie Fenton in your English class. Now your teacher has asked you to write an essay answering these questions:

     How does Julie Fenton feel at the end of the book, and why?

     Write your **essay**.

  (b) *Pride and Prejudice* by Jane Austen
     This is part of a letter you have received from your friend Nathan.

> *I really enjoyed the book but I don't understand why it is called 'Pride and Prejudice'.*
> *What do you think? Write and tell me.*   *Nathan*

     Write your **letter** to Nathan.

PAPER 3   USE OF ENGLISH (45 minutes)

Part 1

For questions **1–12**, read the text below and decide which answer (**A, B, C** or **D**) best fits each gap. There is an example at the beginning (**0**).

Mark your answers **on the separate answer sheet**.

Example:

0   A priceless   **B** rewarding   **C** precious   **D** prized

0	A	B	C	D
	—	▬	—	—

Mountain climbing

One of the most difficult but **(0)** ..... of pastimes is mountain climbing. The modern climber must **(1)** ..... many different skills. Rock climbing **(2)** ..... a combination of gymnastic ability, imagination and observation, but perhaps the most necessary skill is being able to **(3)** ..... out how much weight a particular rock will **(4)** ..... . Mountaineers climb in groups of three or four, each climber at a distance of approximately six metres from the next. Usually one person climbs while the other climbers **(5)** ..... hold of the rope. The most experienced climber goes first and **(6)** ..... the other climbers which way to go, making the rope secure so that it is **(7)** ..... for the others to follow.

With much mountain climbing, snow skills **(8)** ..... a very important part. Ice axes are used for **(9)** ..... steps into the snow and for testing the ground. Climbers always tie themselves together so that, if the leader falls, he or she can be held by the others and **(10)** ..... back to safety. The number of dangers **(11)** ..... by climbers is almost endless. And the **(12)** ..... of oxygen at high altitudes makes life even more difficult for mountaineers.

1 **A** own   **B** hold   **C** control   **D** possess

2 **A** requires   **B** insists   **C** calls   **D** orders

3 **A** work   **B** try   **C** stand   **D** set

4 **A** supply   **B** provide   **C** support   **D** offer

5 **A** keep   **B** stay   **C** continue   **D** maintain

6 **A** indicates   **B** signals   **C** points   **D** shows

7 **A** safe   **B** sure   **C** dependable   **D** reliable

8 **A** act   **B** do   **C** play   **D** make

9 **A** cutting   **B** tearing   **C** breaking   **D** splitting

10 **A** given   **B** pulled   **C** put   **D** sent

11 **A** marked   **B** touched   **C** felt   **D** faced

12 **A** need   **B** gap   **C** lack   **D** demand

Part 2

For questions **13–24**, read the text below and think of the word which best fits each gap. Use only **one** word in each gap. There is an example at the beginning (**0**).

Write your answers **IN CAPITAL LETTERS on the separate answer sheet**.

Example: | **0** | | O | F | | | | | | | | | | | | | | | | | | |

A new cruise ship

One **(0)** ...*of*.... the biggest passenger ships in history, the *Island Princess*, carries people on cruises around the Caribbean. More than double **(13)** .... weight of the *Titanic* (the large passenger ship which sank in 1912), it was **(14)** .... large to be built in **(15)** .... piece. Instead, 48 sections **(16)** .... total were made in different places. The ship was then put together at a shipbuilding yard in Italy.

The huge weight of the *Island Princess* is partly due to her enormous height, **(17)** .... is an incredible 41 metres. When compared with the *Titanic*, she is also a much broader ship. As **(18)** .... as length is concerned, there's little difference – the *Island Princess* is over 250 metres long, similar to the length of the *Titanic*.

The *Island Princess* can carry **(19)** .... to 2,600 passengers and has 1,321 cabins, including 25 specially designed **(20)** .... use by disabled passengers. There is entertainment on board to suit **(21)** .... age and interest, from dancing to good drama. The *Island Princess* seems very likely to be a popular holiday choice for many years to **(22)** .... , even though most people will **(23)** .... to save up in order to be **(24)** .... to afford the trip.

Part 3

For questions **25–34**, read the text below. Use the word given in capitals at the end of some of the lines to form a word that fits in the gap **in the same line**. There is an example at the beginning (**0**).

Write your answers **IN CAPITAL LETTERS on the separate answer sheet**.

Example: | **0** | A | N | X | I | E | T | Y | | | | | | | | | | |

Float your troubles away

Nowadays, anyone who is trying to ease pain or reduce their level

of **(0)** ....*anxiety*........ can try a treatment which is known as flotation   **ANXIOUS**

therapy. Experts have claimed that this can **(25)** .... a significant   **RELIEF**

number of medical conditions. The patient is asked to lie **(26)** .... in   **MOTION**

a large tank, which is filled with warm, salty water. When the

patient is in the water, it is so **(27)** .... that he or she becomes   **PEACE**

(28) .... relaxed.   **EXTREME**

As well as being of **(29)** .... value in dealing with the patient's mental   **PRACTICE**

state, flotation is said to lead to a reduction in high blood **(30)** ....   **PRESS**

and to ease long-term physical pain. Even people whose level of

(31) .... is said to be good are certain to find that it is worth taking   **FIT**

the time to float. Studies have shown that the therapy can be of

considerable **(32)** .... in giving up smoking, losing weight and   **ASSIST**

finding effective **(33)** .... to difficult problems. All of this is achieved   **SOLVE**

by the simple method of freeing the patient's brain from the many

(34) .... aspects of everyday life. In future years, this may become   **PLEASANT**

a standard method of dealing with stress-related problems.

Part 4

For questions **35–42**, complete the second sentence so that it has a similar meaning to the first sentence, using the word given. **Do not change the word given**. You must use between **two** and **five** words, including the word given.

Example:

0   You must do exactly what the manager tells you.

CARRY

You must .... instructions exactly.

The gap can be filled by the words 'carry out the manager's', so you write:

| Example: | 0 | *CARRY OUT THE MANAGER'S* |

Write **only** the missing words **IN CAPITAL LETTERS on the separate answer sheet**.

---

35   As a result of the strong wind last night, several tiles came off the roof.

BECAUSE

Several tiles came off the roof .... so strong last night.

36   Simona last wrote to me seven months ago.

HEARD

I .... Simona for seven months.

37   I don't recommend hiring skis at this shop.

ADVISABLE

It's .... skis at this shop.

38   Mike's father started the company that Mike now runs.

SET

The company that Mike now runs .... his father.

39 The number of car owners has risen over the past five years.

RISE

Over the past five years, there .... in the number of car owners.

40 Naomi said that she would never talk to anyone else about the matter.

DISCUSS

Naomi promised never .... anyone else.

41 'This is the best hotel I've ever stayed in,' my colleague said.

NEVER

'I've .... hotel than this,' my colleague said.

42 There were very few people at the concert last night.

CAME

Hardly .... the concert last night.

PAPER 4   LISTENING (approximately 40 minutes)

Part 1

You will hear people talking in eight different situations. For questions **1–8**, choose the best answer (**A**, **B** or **C**).

---

1   On a train, you overhear a woman phoning her office.
Why has she phoned?

   A   to check the time of an appointment

   B   to apologise for being late

   C   to find out where her diary is

2   You switch on the radio in the middle of a programme.
What kind of programme is it?

   A   a nature programme

   B   a cookery programme

   C   a news programme

3   You overhear a conversation between a watchmaker and a customer.
What does the watchmaker say about the watch?

   A   It is impossible to repair it.

   B   It is not worth repairing.

   C   He does not have the parts to repair it.

4   You overhear a woman talking about her new neighbours.
How does she feel?

   A   offended

   B   shocked

   C   suspicious

5 You hear a man talking about deep-sea diving.
  Why does he like the sport?

  A It suits his sociable nature.

  B It contrasts with his normal lifestyle.

  C It fulfils his need for a challenge in life.

6 You turn on the radio and hear a scientist being interviewed about violins.
  What is the scientist doing?

  A explaining how a violin works

  B explaining how a violin is made

  C explaining how a violin should be played

7 You hear part of a radio programme about CD-ROMs.
  What is the speaker's opinion of the CD-ROMs about Australia which she tried?

  A Most of them are disappointing.

  B You are better off with an ordinary guidebook.

  C There is little difference between them.

8 You turn on the radio and hear a woman giving advice to business people.
  What advice does she give about dealing with customers?

  A Don't let them force you to agree to something.

  B Don't be too sympathetic towards them.

  C Don't allow them to stay on the phone too long.

Part 2

You will hear part of a radio programme in which a woman called Sylvia Short is interviewed about her job. For questions **9–18**, complete the sentences.

Sylvia studied | *and* | **9** | at university.

After university, Sylvia worked as a | | **10** | in Italy.

The company which employs Sylvia is called | | **11**

Sylvia worked for the company for

| | **12** | before becoming the manager's assistant.

Part of Sylvia's job is to organise the

| | **13** | in newspapers and magazines.

Sylvia often has to deal with strange questions from | | **14**

Sylvia's boss has a radio show on Fridays on the subject of

| | **15**

Sylvia has written about her | | **16** | for a new book on Britain.

Sylvia says that in the future she would like to be a

| | **17** | on television.

Last year, Sylvia enjoyed attending a | | **18** | in Australia.

Part 3

You will hear five different people speaking on the subject of motorbikes. For questions **19–23**, choose the phrase (**A–F**) which best summarises what each speaker is talking about. Use the letters only once. There is one extra letter which you do not need to use.

A the perfect passenger

| | Speaker 1 | | 19 |

B a feeling of power

| | Speaker 2 | | 20 |

C a lengthy career

| | Speaker 3 | | 21 |

D the best way to learn

| | Speaker 4 | | 22 |

E a family business

| | Speaker 5 | | 23 |

F a break with routine

Part 4

You will hear part of a radio interview with Steve Thomas, a young chef who has his own cookery series on television. For questions **24–30**, choose the best answer (**A, B** or **C**).

24 On his TV programme, Steve likes to show audiences

   A   the process of cooking.

   B   amusing incidents.

   C   attractively presented dishes.

25 Steve was given his own TV series because

   A   he cooked for a TV company.

   B   he appeared on a TV programme.

   C   he had been recommended to a TV producer.

26 What made him take up cooking as a child?

   A   His parents expected him to help in their restaurant.

   B   He felt it was the best way of getting some money.

   C   His father wanted to teach him to cook.

27 How did Steve feel once he got to college?

   A   He still found academic work difficult.

   B   He regretted not studying harder at school.

   C   He was confident about his practical work.

28 What does Steve say about the cooks who work for him?

   A   He is sometimes unfair to them.

   B   He demands a lot from them.

   C   He trains them all himself.

29 Steve admires Ron Bell because

    A   he prepares traditional dishes.

    B   he writes excellent articles about food.

    C   he makes a point of using local produce.

30 How will Steve's book be different from other books about cooking?

    A   the varieties of food it deals with

    B   the way that it is illustrated

    C   the sort of person it is aimed at

PAPER 5　SPEAKING (14 minutes)

You take the Speaking test with another candidate, referred to here as your partner. There are two examiners. One will speak to you and your partner and the other will be listening. Both examiners will award marks.

Part 1 (3 minutes)

The examiner asks you and your partner questions about yourselves. You may be asked about things like 'your home town', 'your interests', 'your career plans', etc.

Part 2 (a one-minute 'long turn' for each candidate, plus 20-second response from the second candidate)

The examiner gives you two photographs and asks you to talk about them for one minute. The examiner then asks your partner a question about your photographs and your partner responds briefly.

Then the examiner gives your partner two different photographs. Your partner talks about these photographs for one minute. This time the examiner asks you a question about your partner's photographs and you respond briefly.

Part 3 (approximately 3 minutes)

The examiner asks you and your partner to talk together. You may be asked to solve a problem or try to come to a decision about something. For example, you might be asked to decide the best way to use some rooms in a language school. The examiner gives you a picture to help you but does not join in the conversation.

Part 4 (approximately 4 minutes)

The examiner asks some further questions, which leads to a more general discussion of what you have talked about in Part 3. You may comment on your partner's answers if you wish.

UNIVERSITY *of* **CAMBRIDGE**
ESOL Examinations

SAMPLE

Candidate Name
If not already printed, write name
in CAPITALS and complete the
Candidate No. grid (in pencil).

Centre No.

Candidate Signature ....

Candidate No.

Examination Title

Examination Details

Centre

Supervisor:

If the candidate is ABSENT or has WITHDRAWN shade here ▭

Candidate No. grid:
0 0 0 0
1 1 1 1
2 2 2 2
3 3 3 3
4 4 4 4
5 5 5 5
6 6 6 6
7 7 7 7
8 8 8 8
9 9 9 9

Candidate Answer Sheet

Instructions

Use a PENCIL (B or HB).

Mark ONE letter for each question.

For example, if you think B is the right answer to the question, mark your answer sheet like this:

0 A B C D E F G H

Rub out any answer you wish to change using an eraser.

1	A B C D E F G H
2	A B C D E F G H
3	A B C D E F G H
4	A B C D E F G H
5	A B C D E F G H
6	A B C D E F G H
7	A B C D E F G H
8	A B C D E F G H
9	A B C D E F G H
10	A B C D E F G H
11	A B C D E F G H
12	A B C D E F G H
13	A B C D E F G H
14	A B C D E F G H
15	A B C D E F G H
16	A B C D E F G H
17	A B C D E F G H
18	A B C D E F G H
19	A B C D E F G H
20	A B C D E F G H

21	A B C D E F G H
22	A B C D E F G H
23	A B C D E F G H
24	A B C D E F G H
25	A B C D E F G H
26	A B C D E F G H
27	A B C D E F G H
28	A B C D E F G H
29	A B C D E F G H
30	A B C D E F G H
31	A B C D E F G H
32	A B C D E F G H
33	A B C D E F G H
34	A B C D E F G H
35	A B C D E F G H
36	A B C D E F G H
37	A B C D E F G H
38	A B C D E F G H
39	A B C D E F G H
40	A B C D E F G H

Sample answer sheet: Paper 3

UNIVERSITY *of* CAMBRIDGE
ESOL Examinations

S A M P L E

Candidate Name
If not already printed, write name
in CAPITALS and complete the
Candidate No. grid (in pencil).

Candidate Signature

Examination Title

Centre

Supervisor:
If the candidate is ABSENT or has WITHDRAWN shade here ▭

Centre No.

Candidate No.

Examination
Details

0	0	0	0
1	1	1	1
2	2	2	2
3	3	3	3
4	4	4	4
5	5	5	5
6	6	6	6
7	7	7	7
8	8	8	8
9	9	9	9

Candidate Answer Sheet

Instructions
Use a PENCIL (B or HB). Rub out any answer you wish to change using an eraser.

Part 1: Mark ONE letter for each question.

For example, if you think **B** is the right
answer to the question, mark your
answer sheet like this:　0　A　B̶　C　D

Parts 2, 3 and **4:** Write your answer clearly
in CAPITAL LETTERS.

For Parts 2 and 3 write one letter
in each box. For example:

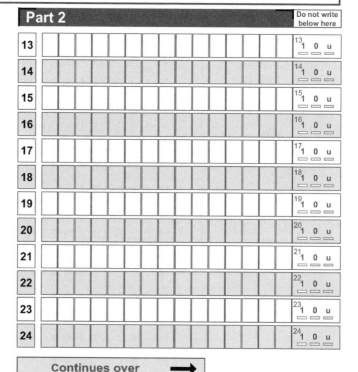

Part 1

1	A	B	C	D
2	A	B	C	D
3	A	B	C	D
4	A	B	C	D
5	A	B	C	D
6	A	B	C	D
7	A	B	C	D
8	A	B	C	D
9	A	B	C	D
10	A	B	C	D
11	A	B	C	D
12	A	B	C	D

Part 2

Do not write
below here

13, 14, 15, 16, 17, 18, 19, 20, 21, 22, 23, 24

Continues over ➡

Part 3

		Do not write below here
25		25 1 0 u
26		26 1 0 u
27		27 1 0 u
28		28 1 0 u
29		29 1 0 u
30		30 1 0 u
31		31 1 0 u
32		32 1 0 u
33		33 1 0 u
34		34 1 0 u

Part 4

		Do not write below here
35		35 2 1 0 u
36		36 2 1 0 u
37		37 2 1 0 u
38		38 2 1 0 u
39		39 2 1 0 u
40		40 2 1 0 u
41		41 2 1 0 u
42		42 2 1 0 u

Sample answer sheet: Paper 4

UNIVERSITY *of* CAMBRIDGE
ESOL Examinations

S A M P L E

Candidate Name
If not already printed, write name
in CAPITALS and complete the
Candidate No. grid (in pencil).

Candidate Signature

Examination Title

Centre

Supervisor:

If the candidate is ABSENT or has WITHDRAWN shade here ▭

Centre No.

Candidate No.

**Examination
Details**

Test version: A B C D E F J K L M N   Special arrangements: S H

Candidate Answer Sheet

Instructions

Use a PENCIL (B or HB).
Rub out any answer you wish to change using an eraser.

Parts 1, 3 and **4:**
Mark ONE letter for each question.

For example, if you think **B** is the
right answer to the question, mark
your answer sheet like this:

Part 2:
Write your answer clearly in CAPITAL LETTERS.

Write one letter or number in each box.
If the answer has more than one word, leave one
box empty between words.

For example:

Turn this sheet over to start.

© UCLES 2009 Photocopiable

98

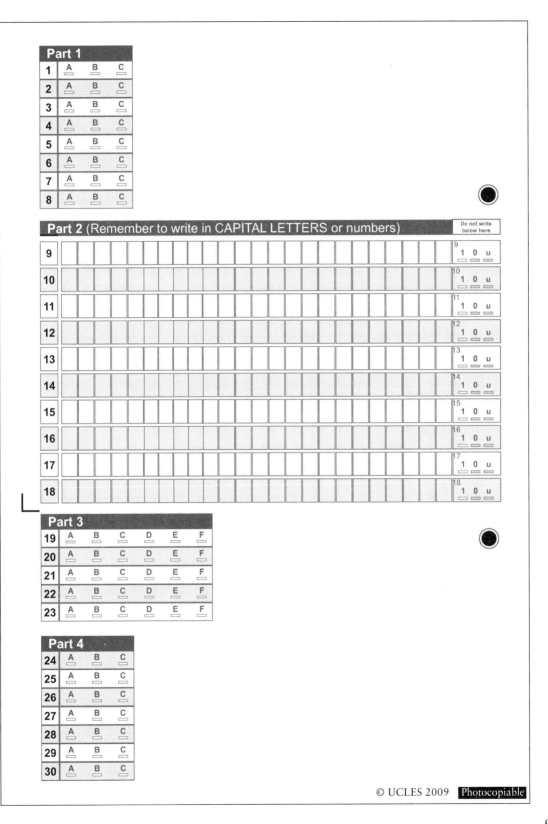